# TRUE STORIES OF
# CRIME &
# DETECTION

First published in 2003 by Usborne Publishing Ltd,
Usborne House, 83-85 Saffron Hill,
London EC1N 8RT, England.
www.usborne.com

A catalogue record for this title is available
from the British Library.

ISBN 07945 06135

Printed in Great Britain

Additional material by Henry Brook
Designed by Sarah Cronin
Series editors: Jane Chisholm and Rosie Dickins
Series designer: Mary Cartwright
Cover design by Glen Bird
Cover photograph © Eigo Shimojo

# TRUE STORIES OF
# CRIME &
# DETECTION

## GILL HARVEY

# CONTENTS

# The man of
# many disguises

Crime is as old as human beings. Every society has rules about how to behave, and there are always some people who decide to break them. As a result, there have been police forces, courtrooms and judges since the days of ancient civilizations. But, strange as it may seem, there haven't always been detectives. No one thought of using specialist skills for tracking down criminals until early in the 19th century. Then, it took just one extraordinary French criminal to change everything. His name was Jean-François Vidocq.

Vidocq was never a bad man. He wasn't the sort to rob unsuspecting people, or murder innocent men. But when he was young he was full of high spirits, and this often got him into trouble. He loved the high life: fencing, gambling, and fighting with other men over women. He adopted daring disguises and, for a while, he even claimed (falsely) to be a captain in the army. Sooner or later, he was bound to get arrested… and sure enough, after one particular brawl, that is exactly what happened.

Vidocq was sent to jail for three months. It was just a local jail, and he would have been fine if he had minded his own business. But that wasn't Vidocq's way. He felt sorry for a peasant who had been wrongly convicted, and helped some other prisoners to forge a letter of release, granting the peasant his freedom.

The trick worked – at first. The peasant was released, but it didn't take long for the authorities to work out what had happened. Forgery was a serious crime, and this time, in 1798, Vidocq was sent to the "galleys".

The galleys were terrible places, designed to punish the most hardened criminals. Prisoners were kept in squalid conditions, chained together, and were forced to do backbreaking physical work on a diet of slops. If they didn't obey, they were beaten viciously. Many didn't survive the experience, and, with a sentence of eight years, Vidocq knew he had a simple choice: escape or die.

Escaping the galleys was no easy task, however. In fact, it was almost impossible. But Vidocq was clever and determined. Gradually, he smuggled in parts of a sailor's uniform, and used a file to cut through his chains. Then, one day, as the chained men marched through the town, Vidocq slipped away… to freedom.

His freedom didn't last for long. He had no papers, and a year later he was recognized as an escapee from the galleys. So, in 1799, he was sent back – this time for sixteen years. He felt desperate, but set to work on a plan for escape once again. It wasn't long before he managed to get hold of another sailor's disguise, and bribed a guard to give him removable chains. He awaited his chance, and took it boldly – just as he'd done the last time. Leaving the town wasn't easy without papers, but Vidocq's craftiness came to the rescue. He pretended to join a funeral, and marched solemnly with the other mourners to the cemetery outside the city gates. Then, he walked free again.

So, at the age of only twenty-three, Vidocq was famous among criminals. It was impressive to escape the galleys once – but twice! This was almost beyond belief, and his fellow criminals regarded him as a hero. But this didn't make his life any easier. The authorities were still hunting for him, and it was difficult to survive without falling deeper into a life of crime.

Sure enough, trouble wasn't far off. He joined up with a group of violent robbers for protection, but when he refused to work with them, they betrayed him. To his dismay, he was soon back in the hands of the authorities in the French town of Lyons.

But this time, something changed. The chief of police, a man named Monsieur Dubois, could see that Vidocq was made of unusual stuff. He offered him a choice.

"You can go back to the galleys," he told Vidocq. "Or you can give me the names of some of your criminal friends."

For Vidocq, the choice was easy. He had no great love of being a criminal – he had never done anything badly wrong. And he certainly didn't want to go back to the galleys. He gave M. Dubois the information he wanted.

Technically, though, Vidocq was still a criminal. M. Dubois might have released him for now, but he still had the conviction for forgery hanging over him. And he was constantly meeting fellow criminals who wanted to involve him in their activities. Vidocq was fed up with the whole situation, and so he devised a plan. If he wanted to make a fresh start, he would need a pardon for his previous crime so that he was no longer a wanted man. And so, in exchange for a full pardon for the forgery, and protection from the police, he moved to Paris and became a secret informer on a regular basis.

Being an informer was an ideal role for Vidocq. He hadn't lost his knack for disguises, and the criminal underworld trusted him. He was one of them, wasn't he? Before long, he was giving the police more information than they could have dreamed possible – and the criminals themselves had no idea how the pilce could know so much. Vidocq was enjoying himself. He was free at last, and he'd found a career.

Whatever he did, Vidocq did with passion, commitment and ingenuity. It wasn't enough for him to pass on casually what he knew; before long, he was actually using his genius to hunt down criminals. The informer became a detective – the first the world had ever seen.

On a personal level, Vidocq was not only the first, but probably the greatest, detective too. He continued to use disguises throughout his life – the same ones, for years and years; but no one ever saw through them. He sometimes went around as an old man called Jean-Louis, a Breton who dealt in stolen goods. At other times, he was Jules, a bearded war veteran with a limp. When he adopted these disguises, he changed everything: the way he spoke, the way he looked, even the way he ate. He understood one of the most important principles of detective work – attention to detail.

By 1811, his work was so successful that he was employing other agents to help him. They were all ex-criminals like himself, because Vidocq claimed that only they had enough knowledge to infiltrate the underworld; and besides, it was only them that he fully trusted. And he pestered the police to give him his own special department, which would be responsible for tracking down crime across the entire city of Paris. In 1812, he got his way at last. He established the Sûreté, the world's first secret security service.

The whole setup of the Sûreté was new. It was a city-wide investigation force, unlike the local police departments that had existed before; and it used plain clothes agents, who were much more effective at detecting crime than police in uniform. But the particular methods developed by Vidocq were even more revolutionary. He taught his agents how to watch people, to notice details, and to think them through. He also understood that there was no point in arresting someone unless you could prove what he'd done.

"To catch criminals, you must be observant," he would say. "You must look at things carefully. You may be surprised at what they show you. Then, when you notice something interesting, write it down. That way, you won't forget – and you will have provided evidence for later."

One of his earliest and best-known cases illustrated Vidocq's principles in action. He was constantly befriending people who led a criminal lifestyle, with the intention of catching them. One of these was a thief named Hotot. Vidocq and an agent dropped in on him one morning to say hello. Hotot seemed tired. His clothes were wet and his boots were muddy – hardly the condition of a man who'd just spent a comfortable night in bed.

*Hmm*, thought Vidocq to himself. *I suspect he's had a busy night.*

Leaving Hotot to rest, he went to find out if there

had been any major burglaries the night before. Sure enough, there had been one in the area, and Vidocq set off immediately to inspect the site.

"Look," he said to his colleagues, as they wandered around. "See those boot prints? They must have been made by one of the thieves."

In the back of his mind, he thought of Hotot's muddy boots. He turned to one of his agents. "Fetch some plaster of Paris," he instructed him. "Pour it into one of these prints to make a plaster cast."

Leaving the agent with this task, he went back to Hotot's place with plenty of wine, and soon the thief was so drunk that he didn't notice another agent slip away with his muddy boots. Later that day, Vidocq received the news he expected: the plaster cast of the prints matched Hotot's boots perfectly. And how could Hotot deny evidence like that? He was tried, and sent to the galleys.

As well as having a sharp sense of observation, Vidocq was intelligent enough to piece a crime together from scraps of information – just as all the great fictional detectives are famous for doing.

The case came up of a butcher named Fontaine, who had been robbed, badly beaten and stabbed on a dark, lonely road. By some miracle, he had survived, and had given an account of his ordeal. He had been on his way to market, and had stopped at an inn for a drink. There, he met two strangers, and started chatting.

"I'm not keen on walking further in the dark," he told them. "I'm carrying money to buy beasts at the market. I wouldn't want to be robbed."

"We'll walk with you," offered the men.

"Would you?" said Fontaine gratefully.

"Of course," said his new friends.

So off they set.

But these "friends" soon turned nasty. They led Fontaine the wrong way, then beat him, stabbed him and took all his money. They left him for dead.

Fontaine was able to give the police a description of the men, and of what they were wearing. "I put up a good fight," he told them. "I knocked one of them to his knees, and he came down with a nice crunch."

The police visited the scene of the crime, and found a scrap of paper. After this, the case was handed to Vidocq. The police gave him the butcher's account of the events, and handed him the scrap of paper.

Vidocq studied the paper carefully. This is what it said:

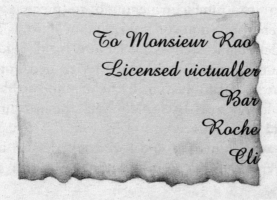

*To Monsieur Rao*
*Licensed victualler*
*Bar*
*Roche*
*Cli*

It didn't take Vidocq long to work out that the paper was addressed to Monsieur Raoul, a wine merchant on the Clignancourt Road, at the Barriere Rochechouart. Raoul was a smuggler with an ugly reputation. Vidocq knew him well. He set up spies outside his shop and, remembering what the butcher had said, told them to look out for anyone who seemed to have damaged his knee.

They didn't have to wait long. There was a Monsieur Court who came and went - and who seemed to be having problems walking. What was more, his clothes matched the description given by the butcher. Vidocq decided to pay him a visit.

"I've been told you're involved in smuggling," Vidocq told him, when Court answered the door. "I need to take a look around."

Monsieur Court looked relieved at the mention of smuggling, and allowed Vidocq into his home. There, Vidocq soon found what he was looking for - weapons, and some freshly washed clothes. Too late, Court realized he'd been tricked, and Vidocq arrested him. Then he went to find Raoul.

Just as he'd done with Court, Vidocq first put Raoul at ease.

"We've been told you're holding anti-government meetings here, and that you have a load of leaflets," he told the scoundrel.

Raoul grinned. "You can take a look," he said, and gave Vidocq the key to his desk.

There, Vidocq came across a letter with the corner

torn off. He was quite sure it would match the scrap of paper he'd been handed by the police – and, just like his fellow criminal, Raoul realized his mistake. Seeing the paper in Vidocq's hand, he gave a howl of rage and dived for his pistols… too late. Vidocq's agents arrested him, and he was taken away.

Vidocq was right about the letter. It matched the scrap perfectly. So, with evidence such as this against them, the two men stood little chance. The butcher identified them as the men who had attacked him, and they were sent to the guillotine.

With his powers of deduction, his cunning disguises and his unfailing eye for detail, Vidocq came to be feared and hated by criminals all over France. It seemed that there was no end to his inventiveness. Ideas occurred to him that had never occurred to anyone else. There must be some sure way to identify a criminal, he mused – some way in which each person was unique. How about… fingerprints? Vidocq was sure that if he could find some way of printing them neatly enough, his theory would be shown to be true. So he set to work with chemists to find a suitable ink.

Unfortunately, after countless experiments, all the inks available still smudged the fingerprints too badly. But we now know that Vidocq was right, and that he set detectives on the track of a method that is still used to identify people today. It's something we take for granted – just as we accept that if someone is shot, an autopsy is carried out, and a ballistics (gun) expert is called in… but it wasn't always the case.

In 1822, Comtesse Isabelle d'Arcy, a beautiful countess, was found murdered – shot through the head. It soon became clear that the obvious suspect was her husband. He was much older than her, and it turned out that she had been having an affair with a man named Deloro. So the Comte d'Arcy was arrested and thrown into jail. But there was no evidence at the scene of the crime; convicting the Comte would be tricky, so Vidocq was called in to investigate.

Vidocq was uneasy about the arrest. The Comte didn't seem the type to have carried out such a crime. Besides, his were pistols for duels, and they showed no signs of recent use. So the master detective turned his attentions to the Comtesse's lover instead.

First, though, there was a delicate matter to deal with. Vidocq wanted to take a look at the bullet that had killed the countess – but it was still embedded in her head. He approached a doctor, a friend of his.

"My friend, I'd like you to do something for me," Vidocq explained to him. "Can you get hold of this bullet for me?"

The doctor looked shocked. "But that would mean… cutting open her head," he protested.

"Precisely," said Vidocq.

"I can't defile a body like that!" cried the doctor.

Vidocq smiled gently. "Come now, my friend," he

said. "When she is finally buried, who will be any the wiser?"

The doctor muttered and shook his head, but Vidocq was very persuasive. The doctor got him his bullet.

As Vidocq had suspected, the bullet was far too big for the Count's pistols. It had been shot from a much bigger gun. Vidocq was determined to find it, and Deloro's home was the obvious place to start.

With his usual cunning, Vidocq used a trick to gain entry. Once inside, not only did he find a pistol that could have fired the fatal bullet – he found a stash of the Countess's valuables, too. Deloro's number was up. Faced with the evidence, he confessed that he had killed his lover and robbed her. Like so many criminals in Vidocq's time, he was tried and sent to the guillotine.

Stories about Vidocq are countless. He lived an extravagant, flamboyant life, and became a living legend. He had many literary friends who were more than willing to write about his exploits – famous writers such as Victor Hugo, Honoré de Balzac and Alexandre Dumas all knew him well, and based some of their fictional characters upon him. As a result, there are many tales about Vidocq that are wildly exaggerated, and far too fanciful. But many others were absolutely true.

As the Sûreté became larger and better established, Vidocq demanded salaries for his men, ensuring that the role of detective would become a respectable one for generations to come. In 1813, the force moved beyond Paris; Vidocq was given permission to open offices in Arras, Brest, Toulon and Lyons, some of the biggest cities in France. Then, in 1818, he made the radical move of introducing women agents to his force. Detectives and their methods were here to stay.

# No body,
# no murder

It was the beginning of a very average day at the Onslow Court Hotel in the smart London borough of Kensington.

Mrs. Constance Lane sat down for breakfast in the hotel restaurant, just as she always did day in, day out. There were the sounds of the hotel staff going about their business, and the tranquil chink of cutlery and china as the regulars were enjoying their bacon and eggs.

But, as Mrs. Lane sipped her tea, she noticed with a frown that her friend, Mrs. Durand-Deacon, hadn't come down from her room. *Funny*, she thought to herself. Her friend hadn't appeared for dinner the previous evening, either. Perhaps she'd gone away – but wouldn't she have said?

"Good morning, Mrs. Lane," said one of her fellow residents, as she left the restaurant half an hour later. It was Mr. Haigh, a smart young man who always seemed charming and cheerful, although Mrs. Lane didn't know him well.

"Good morning," responded Mrs. Lane. "Fine morning, isn't it?"

Mr. Haigh nodded. "Yes, yes, very fine indeed."

Mrs. Lane was about to go on up the stairs, but Mr. Haigh seemed keen to talk to her. "I think Mrs. Durand-Deacon must be unwell," he continued. "We'd arranged to go on a trip to Crawley yesterday, but she didn't come to meet me. Have you heard any news of her?"

"No, I haven't," said Mrs. Lane. "To be honest I was wondering where she was myself. I'll go and check with the chambermaid."

She made her way up the stairs of the hotel and found the maid.

"Is Mrs. Durand-Deacon in her room?" she asked.

"No, ma'am. Mrs. Durand-Deacon didn't come back last night," the maid informed her. "Her room hasn't been slept in."

*How very odd*, thought Mrs. Lane. Mrs. Durand-Deacon was a woman of very regular habits. She wasn't the sort of person to leave the hotel overnight without telling anyone. In fact, she'd mentioned her trip to Crawley with Mr. Haigh only the day before. Mrs. Lane had warned her that it was chilly outside, so Mrs. Durand-Deacon had hurried back upstairs for her Persian lamb coat. But, according to Mr. Haigh, she'd never kept the appointment... *very* strange.

Mrs. Lane hurried back downstairs. "She didn't come back last night," she told Mr. Haigh, as he stood in the foyer pulling on his fine yellow kid gloves.

"Well, I'm sure there must be a simple explanation," said Mr. Haigh. "I'm going out. Perhaps she'll be back later. Good day, Mrs. Lane."

But Mrs. Durand-Deacon didn't appear that evening. The next morning, Mr. Haigh came over to Mrs. Lane's breakfast table.

"Any news?" he asked. "I see there's still no sign of her."

"No, nothing at all," said Mrs. Lane. "Quite frankly, I think there's something fishy about it. I'm going to report her disappearance to the police."

Mr. Haigh looked thoughtful. "Perhaps you're right," he said. "It is rather strange." He stroked his chin for a moment, looking full of concern. "I could give you a lift to the police station myself," he suggested. "Shall we go after lunch?"

So it was that the disappearance of Mrs. Durand-Deacon was reported at Chelsea Police Station, London, on February 20, 1949. As far as the police were concerned, there was nothing so very unusual about the disappearance of an old woman. It happened all the time. People went away without telling anyone, and appeared fine and well somewhere else.

Detective Inspector Symes took a statement from Mr. Haigh, and the next day initiated a routine investigation. He summoned one of the women police officers, Police Sergeant Lambourne.

"An old widow's gone missing from the Onslow Court Hotel in Kensington," he informed her. "Would you go and take a look around down there? See if anything comes up."

Sergeant Lambourne nodded, and headed off. Meanwhile, Detective Inspector Symes made an announcement in the press, giving a description and asking the public for any sightings of the old woman.

At the hotel, Sergeant Lambourne questioned people who had known Mrs. Durand-Deacon. Naturally, Mr. Haigh was one of them, and Sergeant Lambourne took an instant dislike to this dapper little man with his hard, glittering eyes. She took down another statement from him, very similar to the one he had made at the police station: he had arranged to take the old lady to Crawley, but she hadn't shown up. He hadn't seen her since.

"And where did you go, when Mrs. Durand-Deacon missed her appointment?" she asked him.

"I came back to the hotel," said Mr. Haigh, with an easy smile.

Sergeant Lambourne frowned. In his earlier statement, Haigh claimed that he'd gone on to Crawley alone. She went back to the police station.

"There's something funny about Haigh," she told her boss. "I'm not sure what it is, but I think we should carry out a few checks on him."

Inspector Symes agreed, and contacted the

Criminal Records Office at Scotland Yard. The results were interesting. John George Haigh was not quite the charming businessman he appeared to be. He was actually a con man who had already served three prison sentences for fraud and theft.

Inspector Symes was beginning to get interested. He decided to check some of Haigh's statement. Haigh had explained that he was a partner in Hurstlea Products Ltd, an engineering firm in Crawley, Sussex, which is where he had planned to take Mrs. Durand-Deacon.

Inspector Symes phoned the West Sussex Police and gave them details of Hurstlea Products. Officers paid a visit to the firm, and interviewed Mr. Jones, the director.

"So Mr. Haigh is your partner?" they asked him.

"No, no, not as such," said Mr. Jones. "I just let him use one of the storerooms. He says he's carrying out a few experiments, you see."

"Can we see this storeroom?" asked the police.

Mr. Jones shook his head apologetically. "I'm afraid it's locked. Mr. Haigh has the only key," he said.

So, once again, Haigh was not quite as he seemed. The plot was thickening. The police left, and arranged to come back later with a warrant to force their way into the storeroom, if necessary.

In the meantime, there had been another development. Thanks to the description of Mrs. Durand-Deacon in the papers, the owners of a jewel shop had come forward. Messrs. Bull of Horsham had received jewels of the kind worn by the widow on the very day she had disappeared. They had been sold to them by a man named 'McLean', but one of the shop assistants recognized the man as a Mr. Haigh, who had sold items to them in the past.

On Saturday, February 26, the West Sussex Police returned to the Crawley storeroom and forced it open. There wasn't very much inside, but what they found was certainly interesting. There was a revolver in a box, which looked as though it had been recently used. There were some big barrels, half-filled with acid. And among some papers there was a dry cleaners' receipt for a fur coat.

The police hurried to the dry cleaners. Things were beginning to come together fast now, for they were handed a Persian lamb coat just like the one worn by Mrs. Durand-Deacon on the day she had disappeared. It was time to make an arrest.

On February 28, 1949, eight days after the widow's disappearance, Detective Inspector Webb of the Chelsea Police Station pulled in outside the Onslow Court Hotel. There, he found Mr. Haigh, who was just on his way out.

"I'd be obliged if you'd come down to the station with me to answer a few more questions," said Inspector Webb pleasantly.

"Must I come right now?" grumbled Haigh. "I've got a meeting with my solicitors."

"I'm sure your solicitors can wait," the Inspector assured him smoothly.

"Very well," said Haigh, with a sigh. "I'm more than willing to help you, as you know."

Once in the police station, the police kept Haigh waiting for a few hours. Then he was questioned by Inspector Symes. "It seems that you had some of Mrs. Durand-Deacon's jewels," said the Inspector. "And her coat, as well. Could you tell me how you got hold of them?"

John Haigh puffed at his cigarette, and frowned. "Well," he said. "To be honest, I've been involved in some blackmail. I can't talk about it without getting other people into trouble. What do you think I should do?"

"That's entirely up to you," said Inspector Symes.

"I see," said Haigh. He lit another cigarette, deep in thought.

Inspector Symes left the room, leaving Haigh with Inspector Webb. Haigh leaned forward and looked Inspector Webb in the eye.

"Tell me frankly," Haigh asked him. "What are the chances of anybody being released from Broadmoor?"

Inspector Webb looked at Haigh strangely, and didn't answer. It was a very revealing question to ask. At that time, murderers were hanged for their actions – unless they were insane; in which case they were sent to Broadmoor. Was Haigh already working out a plea for his actions? If so, *what* actions?

John George Haigh must have seen the tide turning against him. The police had found the jewels, the coat, and the gun. They had searched his premises at Crawley. But there was still no sign of Mrs. Durand-Deacon. Feeling very sure of himself, Haigh suddenly made the most extraordinary declaration.

"Mrs. Durand-Deacon no longer exists," he told Inspector Webb. "She has disappeared completely and no trace of her can ever be found again."

The Inspector stared at him, baffled. "Disappeared!" he exclaimed. "What do you mean?"

"I have destroyed her with acid," Haigh continued calmly. "You will find the sludge which remains at Leopold Road. Every trace has gone." He gave an easy smile. "How can you prove murder if there is no body?"

Inspector Webb took a deep breath. He decided to call in more inspectors. They cautioned Haigh that anything he said could be used as evidence against him. Then, over the course of the next few hours, Haigh gave a detailed statement about the events that had taken place on February 18.

On that day, he claimed, he had met Mrs. Durand-Deacon as planned. She was interested in the manufacture of plastic stick-on fingernails, and he had told her that he was experimenting with different techniques at his factory in Crawley. He drove her to his private storeroom on Leopold Road in his Alvis car, and there, when she had turned away

27

from him, he shot her with the revolver in the back of the head. He took off her coat and jewels and tipped her, head-first, into a forty-gallon tank – but not before carrying out an extraordinary, sinister ritual. According to Haigh's story, he made a cut in her throat with his pocketknife, filled a small glass with blood, and drank it.

Then he went over to the Olde Ancient Priors' Restaurant in Crawley for an egg on toast and a cup of tea. Feeling refreshed, he went back to the storeroom. Everything was ready for the next stage of the operation. Haigh pulled on a gas mask, a rubber coat, apron and gloves. He fetched his store of sulphuric acid and, with the help of a stirrup pump and a rubber hose, began to fill the tank with acid. When he had added enough, he left the body to react, and went for dinner.

He checked on the body later that day, and again the next day, tipping off some sludge onto the ground outside and adding fresh acid to the remains. He took the fur coat to be cleaned before selling it, and took the jewels to Messrs. Bull. He paid off some debts with the money, and then, a few days later, tipped the last of the sludge out onto the ground. He placed the empty tank outside the storeroom.

The police inspectors listened in disbelief – as well they might. Haigh was perfectly calm and matter-of-fact, and seemed to have enjoyed telling his gruesome tale. He took a short break to drink tea with some bread and cheese, and then he continued.

Mrs. Durand-Deacon, he claimed, was not his first victim. The first had been William Donald McSwann, a young man who had become his friend. He killed McSwann in 1944 at a basement apartment on Gloucester Road in London. This was before he'd acquired a gun, so he had hit the man over the head with a blunt weapon. When anyone asked about William, he explained his disappearance by saying he had gone into hiding to avoid being "called up". (At that time, all young men had to serve for a while in the army.) He kept up this act until 1946, when he killed both William's parents, Donald and Amy McSwann, in the same way.

Another two years passed, and Haigh made the acquaintance of a couple named Henderson. By then, he had rented the storeroom at Leopold Road, Crawley. When he decided their time had come, he stole Dr. Henderson's gun and took him on a trip to the storeroom. After shooting him and placing him in an acid tank, he went back for his wife, telling her that her husband had been taken ill. He disposed of her in the same way.

By the time Haigh had finished giving his account, it was late at night. His confession was sensational, and the police could still hardly believe their ears. But they now had a difficult task on their hands. Haigh clearly believed that no murder charge could be made without a body; but surely there was *some* evidence to establish whether he was telling the truth or not? If so, it was up to the police to find it.

The first task was to return to Leopold Road and take a closer look. Forensic scientists found the sludge outside, just as Haigh had described it, and took away half a ton of soil and sludge for examination. They also examined the inside of the store room more carefully, and found some small smatterings of blood on the wall, along with traces of animal fat on the rubber clothing.

But it was the contents of the soil and sludge that clinched the case. After careful sifting, a small pile of items was placed to one side. They were three strange, ridged pebbles, which turned out to be gall stones; eighteen little pieces of bone, which were human bone; a mass of greasy fat, possibly human; the handle of a red plastic handbag; a lipstick container and – the most crucial piece of evidence of all – a pair of well-preserved dentures.

The dentures were taken to Mrs. Durand-Deacon's dentist. It just so happened that the widow had experienced a number of problems with her gums, and her dentist had taken a plaster cast of her upper and lower jaws. There was no doubt about it: the dentures belonged to Mrs. Durand-Deacon.

Other pieces of evidence gradually came together to confirm Haigh's account of the widow's death. In her room, scraps of a fur coat were found, matching the coat found at the dry cleaners'. The blood on the walls of the store room was proved to be human; the bones in the sludge were those of an elderly woman; and the rest of the handbag was found, and was identified by Mrs. Lane as the bag carried by Mrs. Durand-Deacon on the day she left the hotel for the last time.

As the police carried out their work, Haigh made another announcement.

"I've got something else to tell you," he informed the police. "I killed a middle-aged woman from Hammersmith. That was after I'd killed William McSwann. Then there was Max, from Kensington. I killed him in the autumn of 1945. And, after the Hendersons, I killed a young woman named Mary from Eastbourne. That makes nine in total, doesn't it?"

The police took down Haigh's statement, but treated it with suspicion. They hadn't forgotten Haigh's question about Broadmoor. There he was, sitting awaiting trial on his own with plenty of time to think up fantastic stories. Why hadn't he mentioned these three murders before? He offered very little information about the victims, and gave no motive for killing them, financial or otherwise. Was he just trying to make himself look all the more insane?

When Haigh was officially charged on March 2, 1949, it was only for the murder of Mrs. Durand-Deacon. The police had investigated his story concerning his other victims, and it seemed likely that he had indeed killed the McSwanns and the Hendersons. The evidence was never brought to court, but no trace of these people was ever found after the dates of their alleged murders. And, it turned out, the motive appeared to be money. Haigh had profited handsomely from their disappearance. In the case of the McSwanns, he had forged a number of letters and documents that placed all their property in his hands. This included four houses (which Haigh sold for a fine sum), investments, and all their household goods. Altogether, he probably made about £4,000 – a lot of money in the 1940s.

But Haigh squandered the profits, and it was only when he was hard up again that he turned his attention to the Hendersons. From them, he profited even more, probably notching up about £7,000. But he was a spendthrift, and by the time he befriended Mrs. Durand-Deacon, he was broke all over again.

When Haigh eventually came to trial in July 1949, no one doubted that he was a murderer. After all, he had admitted it himself, and there was plenty of evidence. So it was just a case of working out whether he was insane – or rather, whether he understood that what he had done was wrong.

The only thing to suggest that he was mentally ill was his account of drinking his victims' blood. As his case drew closer to trial, he talked about this more and more, and began to talk about his strange, disturbed dreams – dreams in which wooden crosses dripped with blood and gradually turned into trees. It was his thirst for blood, he claimed, that had led him to kill. Not the money.

But few believed that this was his real motive. His murder of Mrs. Durand-Deacon had been meticulously planned and carried out. He had immediately sold her coat and jewels to sort out his debts. And there was no evidence at all for the blood-drinking that he claimed had taken place.

When all the evidence had been presented, the jury was offered a choice. They could find Haigh "Guilty", or "Guilty but Insane". They took only fifteen minutes to make up their minds. John George Haigh, they said, was guilty of murder, pure and simple.

The judge sentenced Haigh to death, and the "Acid Bath Murderer" was hanged at Wandsworth Prison, in London, on August 6, 1949.

# The embittered artist

"So, Mr. van Meegeren, where exactly did you buy this painting?" asked the Dutch police investigator, in a polite voice.

Han van Meegeren looked the policeman up and down, then smiled. "From an old Italian family, before the war," he replied.

The police investigator looked interested. "An Italian family, you say? Could you please give us the family's name, for our investigations?"

The artist shook his head. "I'm afraid I can't do that," he said, in a regretful tone. "You see, they were such an old, respected family, and they didn't want people to know they'd fallen on hard times. They made me swear I'd never reveal that they'd been selling off their art collection."

The police investigator rubbed his chin. "I see," he said. "That's understandable. But we are going to need their name, all the same. It's rather important."

Han van Meegeren began to get annoyed. "I've told you," he snapped. "I made a promise. I'm not telling you anything."

"Hmm," said the police investigator. "Well, look at it like this. An old Dutch master leaves an Italian family just before the war, and ends up in the collection of a German Nazi officer. Not just any old officer, but Field Marshal Goering himself. We would very much like to speak to this Italian family, don't you see? We shall have to look into their political history."

"Political history!" shouted Han van Meegeren. He stared at the policemen, furious. Too late, he began to see what they were looking for…

It was May 1945, shortly after the end of the Second World War. The Germans and Italians had been defeated, their Fascist regimes at last toppled by the Allied forces. Across Europe, investigations were being carried out to dig out traitors and make the guilty pay for the terrors that they had inflicted. Holland was no exception. The Dutch were on the hunt for anyone who might have betrayed their country and collaborated with the enemy.

In the course of the war, the Nazi occupiers had acquired as many great paintings as they could - paintings that rightfully belonged to other nations. Holland had done everything in its power to protect its masterpieces, but one had slipped through the net and ended up in Field Marshal Goering's collection. It was *The Woman Taken In Adultery*, by 17th-century Dutch master, Johannes Vermeer.

For this to have happened, someone must have

betrayed their country. It just wasn't possible for major works of art to end up in Nazi hands otherwise. The Dutch investigators had traced the sale of the painting back through two agents to this artist, Han van Meegeren. Now, with his casual reference to an Italian family, it seemed that they had found the treacherous link: the artist must have acted as an intermediary between Italian and German fascists. The next day, Han van Meegeren was arrested on the charge of collaboration.

Han van Meegeren knew his moment had come. He was not a collaborator; the accusation horrified him. But to prove his innocence, he was going to have to reveal an extraordinary secret – a secret that would cause a sensation, and one he had been hiding for years.

From an early age, Henri van Meegeren, usually known as Han, had wanted to be a painter. He was always drawing or sketching, rather than doing his schoolwork. His father despaired of him, and when the time came, he insisted that Han should train to become an architect at the University of Delft.

Han was happy enough with this decision. He could leave home at last and be free to paint and draw as much as he liked. It was also an opportunity to meet other people with similar interests, and after a while he met a young woman named Anna de Voogt. Anna was an art student, and soon discovered Han's passion for drawing and painting. She was impressed.

"An architect. What a waste!" she said to him. "You're so talented, Han. You should become an artist."

"Do you really think so?" said Han, feeling pleased and flattered.

"I do," said Anna firmly.

The two young dreamers fell in love, and soon Anna became Han's wife. Han's father was very annoyed, especially when Han abandoned his plans to become an architect. But there was little he could do – Han was determined. He would make a living by selling his work as an artist.

In the early years, Han had quite a lot of success. While he was still a student, he worked exceptionally hard to paint a picture for the Hague Academy Gold Medal competition. It was of the inside of a Gothic church in Rotterdam, and it was magnificent. To his delight, Han won the prize. It was the perfect first step for a young artist, and he was full of hope.

Things continued to move onwards and upwards. The Hague Academy gave Han teaching work, which provided him with a steady income, and he held his first solo exhibition, which was a roaring success. Han managed to sell all his paintings; critics wrote good reviews; and he was approached regularly with commissions for portraits.

Nevertheless, things were not going as well as Han had hoped. For one thing, he was a spendthrift, who lived way beyond his means. He was always in debt, and his relationship with Anna, who now had a child, began to suffer. For another, he was not getting the sort of praise from the critics that he craved. Yes, people liked his portraits and his paintings, but the critics didn't think they were *amazing*. Han was an extremely talented painter, but he had one big problem: he was rather old-fashioned – a traditionalist. This was a time when traditional painting was being attacked on all sides by new, exciting ideas; there had been the Impressionists in the 19th century, followed in the early 20th century by the development of Post-Impressionism, Cubism and Surrealism... artists like Picasso and Dali were the big names, not painters who could turn out work in the traditional style.

This infuriated Han. He despised the new styles and the praise that they received from the critics. More than that, he refused to believe that the critics had any real artistic judgement at all.

"If a painting is good, the critics should say it's good, whoever it's by!" he would fume. "But they don't think like that. They'll ignore a masterpiece by a nobody and praise any stupid sketch if it's scribbled by someone famous!"

There was some truth in this view, for it was partly based on his own experience – for example, in the case of Princess Juliana's deer. This occurred while he was working as a teacher at the Academy. Every week, he obtained the Princess's pet deer as a model for his pupils to paint. One week, as they bent over their work, he quickly sketched the deer himself. It took him only ten minutes, but it was a charming little drawing. A thought popped into Han's head. It would be ideal for publication on Christmas cards and calendars.

He approached a publisher with the sketch, but got no interest.

"Ah, well, never mind," murmured Han. "Though it's a shame. I don't suppose you see many drawings of Princess Juliana's deer."

"Princess Juliana's…?" exclaimed the publisher. "My dear man, why didn't you tell me before? Of course we shall publish it."

Han van Meegeren gave a wry smile, and shrugged. *It's exactly the same drawing, whoever the deer belongs to*, he thought to himself. But armed with this information, the publisher didn't hesitate, and the deer became a well-known sight in Holland on cards, calendars and in magazines.

So, as Han's career inched forward, a seed of bitterness began to grow. Years passed, and still the critics ignored his "best" work. Han was well-liked and popular within artistic circles – always ready for a drink and some fun. But he also attracted scandal, insulted the critics, and neglected his wife and children. He continued to struggle for money, and eventually fell out with Anna completely. In 1923, they were divorced. Meanwhile, Han had fallen in love with the wife of a famous art critic, which provoked another scandal. But Jo de Boer loved Han, too, and the couple eventually married. Even then, Han wasn't really happy, or satisfied with his work.

Gradually, an idea began to take shape in Han's mind. He had always been interested in the works of the Dutch old masters – painters like Vermeer and de Hoogh, and had studied many of the techniques they used. He knew how they made their brilliant pigments from ground-up minerals, and how they applied the paints with badger-hair brushes. Why not forge a 17th-century masterpiece, and fool the critics? He was sure he could do it well enough to make a mockery of their so-called "expertise".

Once the idea took root in his mind, it wouldn't go away, so he began to experiment. One of the most difficult technical problems he had to face was how to make the paint look old enough. It takes fifty years for oil paint to dry thoroughly, but when it has done so, it develops lots of little cracks and becomes completely hard. Not even alcohol will dissolve it. How could Han create the same effect?

He decided that the key would be to bake the painting once it was finished, but even this wasn't straightforward. When he mixed the pigments with ordinary oils, the oils blistered or even caught fire in the oven. On the other hand, if he baked them more gently, the brilliant blues, yellows and whites were spoiled.

Han was patient. For four years, he experimented with different oils and chemicals until, at last, he hit upon a combination that would work. Using lilac oil, and the chemicals phenol and formaldehyde, the paintings did not burn or frizzle up. Even when they were baked at a high temperature, the blues, reds and greens remained as brilliant as ever. He had finally made a breakthrough!

Now very excited, Hans set to work on creating his forgery. He knew that the first thing any critic would check was the canvas itself, so he bought a worthless 17th-century painting called *The Resurrection of Lazarus*. Then he set about carefully scraping off the old paint, so that an X-ray could not reveal it. It was slow work, but at last he was ready to start painting. But what was he going to paint?

The artist Vermeer had not painted very much in his lifetime, and was regarded as the greatest of all the Dutch old masters. His life, and paintings, were shrouded in mystery. It wasn't clear when most of his masterpieces had been painted, or why he hadn't painted more. He was an ideal artist for Han to imitate. He would create a painting that could be attributed to a "mystery period" in Vermeer's life; he could even move away slightly from the obvious Vermeer style and subject matter.

He decided on a religious theme, and began to plan the painting. But he had a problem. Because he was working in absolute secrecy (even his wife had no idea, as Han kept her out of his studio), he could not use a model to base his figures on. But, one day, a poor field worker came begging on his doorstep.

Han saw his opportunity. He took the man in, fed him, and kept him for three days while he worked feverishly on sketches. The poor man was astonished, and enormously grateful. And Han had the material he needed to paint a picture of Christ among his disciples.

*Christ at Emmaus* took Han six months to paint. When he had finished, he added Vermeer's signature in one corner, then baked the painting carefully. He took it out of the oven and stared at it. The blues, reds and yellows were vibrant, and the paints perfectly hard. It was a masterpiece.

Han chuckled to himself. Now all he had to do was create the "crackle" of old paintings, which he did by rolling up the canvas gently until the paint began to crack slightly. Then he blackened the cracks with Indian ink to give the impression of dust and dirt that had built up over the years. The effect was perfect. He had created a painting that was almost impossible to tell apart from a 17th-century original.

The next step was to find some way of selling the painting without revealing his identity. Fortunately for Han, it was quite common for paintings to be sold by go-betweens, and for the owner to remain anonymous. So Han went to visit a solicitor he knew in Paris, thinking he might be happy to act as an agent.

Before he went, he gave a lot of thought to what story he would tell. It was very important to prevent the man from asking too many questions. So he told him that the painting belonged to an old French family, who had received it through a marriage to a Dutch woman, who brought it with her as part of her dowry.

"And you think this painting is valuable?" asked the solicitor, who knew little about the old masters.

"In my opinion, this is a genuine 17th-century painting by Vermeer," said Han. "But it's not really for me to say. To be certain, you must call in the experts."

"Who should I consult?" asked the solicitor. "I don't want to make a fool of myself."

"Dr. Bredius is the recognized authority on the subject," Han told him. "If he says it is a Vermeer, then you can be sure that he is right."

The solicitor accepted this as a wise plan of action, and agreed to contact Dr. Bredius. So Han simply had to wait.

A few days later, he heard the expert's judgement. Dr. Bredius was wildly excited. Not only did he think the painting was most definitely the work of Vermeer – he claimed it was the best the artist had ever painted! The art world was soon buzzing with the news of the new masterpiece. There were mutterings among the critics: could it be a fake? Some thought so. But Dr. Bredius's judgement, revered and respected, carried the day, and the whisperings soon ceased. Now, it was only a matter of time before Han would at last be a rich man.

It was one of the most prestigious museums in Holland, the Boymans Museum, that finally bought the *Christ at Emmaus* for the vast sum of 520,000 guilders (about £58,000 at the time, but much more now). After solicitors' and dealers' fees had been paid, Han was left with about two-thirds of this amount. He went on a wild spending spree, enjoying every minute of his new-found wealth. But what he enjoyed even more was the world-wide excitement at the 'discovery' of the Vermeer. People flocked to the Boymans to admire it, making Han's triumph complete.

Han now faced a momentous decision. Originally, the idea had been to stand up and declare himself the true artist, thus making a fool of all the critics. The chances were that he would be praised for his cleverness, and his own career would surge ahead as a result. But that would mean handing back all the money, and Han was enjoying being rich. What was more, the process of creating the forgery had been so absorbing that Han now felt he had discovered his true talent.

He couldn't resist the temptation. He kept quiet, kept the money, and started work on another. This time, the painting was a fake de Hoogh, another Dutch old master. Once more, he made up a vague story about its origins, and it was accepted as genuine. It made less money than the *Christ at Emmaus*, but it was still a small fortune. Han was now addicted. He painted one more "de Hoogh", then started another "Vermeer". Then another. And another, and another, and another. A total of six "Vermeers", all with a religious theme, in a similar style to the *Christ at Emmaus*. Han was filling in an entire period of the old master's life.

And far from questioning the strange appearance of so many old masterpieces, the art world lapped them up – in spite of the fact that Han painted them more and more carelessly, often not bothering to remove the original paintings from the canvases that he used. No one noticed; no one checked. The prices rose, and Han had so much money he didn't know what to do with it. He bought property – as many as fifty houses; he lived a luxurious lifestyle, threw extraordinarily lavish parties and drank heavily. And still, he told no one the truth, not even his wife. Everyone believed his story: that he had won the National Lottery. Twice!

If it hadn't been for the Second World War, Han's secret might never have been discovered. The majority of his forgeries were painted during the war years, between 1940 and 1944. The last of the Vermeers, *The Woman Taken in Adultery*, had gone for an enormous sum (more than twice the amount paid for *Christ at Emmaus*), and the buyer, two agents down the line from Han, was the German Field Marshal Goering. Up to this point, Han had always refused to sell any paintings to the Germans. But, as his paintings were forgeries, did it really matter? In the course of this final sale, Han added a nice twist. Goering could buy the painting, but he must pay for it with other Dutch paintings and works of art from his collection. Goering agreed – and as a result, more than two hundred genuine Dutch works of art were returned to their rightful homeland.

But it was this that cost Han his secret. In 1945 the Dutch investigators came knocking at his door…

Han was taken into custody and imprisoned for several weeks. He still refused to admit to anything, or to talk about the "Italian family" that he claimed the painting had belonged to. He was getting old and stubborn, and had spent many years carrying the burden of his secret. He wasn't going to let it go so easily.

Then, suddenly, he crumbled.

"Fools!" he shouted at the police. "You're all fools, just like the rest of them! I didn't sell a great national treasure to the Germans. I painted it myself."

The police stared at him, thinking he had gone insane.

"And not just that one, either," continued Han. "I painted *The Head of Christ* and *The Last Supper*, *The Card Players*, *The Drinkers*, *The Footwashing* – all of them. And, what's more, I painted the *Christ at Emmaus* hanging in the Boymans, as well."

There was no stopping him now. Suddenly, the dam had burst and Han wanted everyone to know how he had fooled them for so many years. At first, the police didn't believe him. It sounded too incredible. But, as Han began to talk about his techniques, they began to think he might actually be telling the truth.

"Go and x-ray the paintings!" he told them. "You'll find originals underneath. Well, underneath some of them. I can tell you exactly what the originals were, too."

The police followed his instructions, and found things exactly as Han said they were. But they were still unconvinced. What if Han had taken x-rays of the paintings himself? Then he'd know what lay underneath them anyway. They wanted better proof.

"Mr. van Meegeren," they said, "if you did indeed paint *The Woman Taken in Adultery*, we would like you to demonstrate your skills by painting a copy."

"I'll do better than that," declared Han. "I'll paint an entirely new Vermeer for you, before witnesses."

The police agreed, and for the next few months, Han created an incredible new "Vermeer" before a panel of people, who watched in wonder. As *The Young Christ Teaching in the Temple* began to take shape, the police hurriedly dropped their charge of collaboration.

News of the whole affair began to leak out to the public, and the whole story caused an uproar. The art world was speechless, and the reputation of poor old Dr. Bredius was in tatters. But the matter was not yet over. Although the collaboration charges had been dropped, Han van Meegeren had still committed an enormous crime. The police decided instead to charge him with fraud and forgery, and in June 1946 a commission was set up to gather the evidence.

Han helped the commission willingly and eagerly. He *wanted* to be found guilty; he was desperate to show that he had, after all, been a brilliant artist all these years. The evidence soon piled up. There were other "trial" forgeries in his studio, along with all the materials he claimed to have used. The canvas of *Christ at Emmaus* had been cut down just as Han described. After chemical tests, the paintings were found to contain phenol – a substance unavailable in the 17th century. On close examination, the 'crackle' of the paintings didn't go deep enough, and the 'dirt' lodged in the cracks was, in fact, ink. It all pointed to two things: first, that the paintings could not possibly date from the 17th century; and second, that Han van Meegeren had painted them, as he claimed.

The trial, which opened in October 1947, was a sensation. It delighted the general public, and made the art world squirm. It was shown how careless the so-called experts had been in accepting without question the discovery of so many 'old masters'. Han van Meegeren was, most definitely, guilty. He was sentenced to a year's imprisonment.

He was also bankrupt. The government demanded that he repay all the money he had earned and the tax that was due on it – a monstrous sum that he could not even begin to find. As it happened, he would never have to. The years of deceiving and high living had taken their toll, and Han van Meegeren died on December 30, 1947, only two months after his trial, at the age of 58.

# The American Sherlock Holmes

*Who is the greatest detective the world has ever known? Sherlock Holmes, perhaps? Many people would say so. The problem is that Holmes didn't really exist - he was a fictional character, who only solved crimes in stories. In real life, detectives work as part of a team and it's rare for individuals to become famous. Sometimes, though, one man stands out from the crowd...*

*In the United States in the 1920s, Edward Oscar Heinrich developed an extraordinary reputation as a forensic scientist. He started his career as a chemist in the city of Tacoma in Washington, but his exceptional skills won him the post of Professor of Criminology at Berkeley, part of the University of California. He is said to have solved over 2,000 amazing cases. These are two of the most well-known.*

## The greasy overalls

The long, chugging steam train slowed down slightly as it entered the tunnel, the sound of its whistle echoing back to the passengers.

"Just taking it steady through here," said Sydney Bates, the train engineer, looking around at the fireman.

"Sure, Sydney," said Marvin Seng, taking a moment to pause from loading coal. He and Sydney had completed this journey through the Siskiyou Mountains of Oregon more times than they could remember, but they still liked to chat about their work as they went about it.

Both men looked ahead, staring at the little bright spot of daylight that was gradually growing bigger as the train chuffed towards the end of the tunnel.

Suddenly, they had a big shock.

"Hands up!" bellowed a voice.

Sydney and Marvin froze on the spot. Terrified, they raised their hands slowly into the air. They hadn't seen two men creeping forward into the engine room from the tender, which lay just behind it – not until it was too late.

"Stop the train," instructed one of the intruders. "We want the front end out of the tunnel – as far as the mail car. Leave the rest inside."

With a gun pointing between his ribs, Sydney Bates did as the men said. As the engine nosed into the daylight, he brought it to a halt with a hissing of steam and brakes.

"Get out," ordered the second gunman, pointing his gun at Marvin.

"And you!" snapped the first man at Sydney.

Helpless, the two men jumped down from the

engine doorway, knowing that the guns were pointing at them all the way. The gunmen followed them as they climbed slowly up the hill outside the tunnel's entrance.

"Stop!" yelled one of the gunmen, halfway up the slope.

Sydney and Marvin did as they were told. As they stood looking down at their train, the steam still drifting out of its funnel, they realized that the two gunmen were not alone. There was another man running alongside the mail car, carrying something in his arms. They watched as he attached it to the car, then turned and ran towards them up the hill.

Just as he reached a safe distance from the train, there was an explosion. The mail car disappeared in a cloud of billowing smoke.

"Stop!" exclaimed Sydney, horrified. "Edwin's still inside!"

"Shut up!" growled one of the gunmen.

Sydney and Marvin exchanged looks of desperation. These gunmen, whoever they were, were clearly violent and would stop at nothing. They wondered what had happened to Edwin, the mail clerk. He was the only person actually inside. As the smoke began to clear, they could see a gaping hole in the side – and flames, lapping around the hole and shooting higher as they took control.

"Blast!" shouted the first gunman at the man who had laid the dynamite. "The whole darn thing's on fire! You were only supposed to blow a hole in it, dimwit!" He turned to Sydney. "Get back down there and get the train out of the tunnel!"

Sydney knew better than to resist. He scrambled back down the hill and climbed inside the engine.

"Move it!" bellowed the gunman. He seemed to be getting panicky.

Sydney brought the engine back into life, and tried to shunt it forward. Nothing happened. He gave it more power, but still nothing happened.

"Get on with it!" shrieked the gunman. "What's wrong with you?"

Sydney guessed that the damaged mail car had jammed the whole train to the tracks. "I… I can't," he said faintly, feeling weak with terror.

"*Can't!*" cried the gunman, finally losing his temper. "I'll give you *can't!*"

And those were the last words that Sydney Bates ever heard, because the gunman brought him down in a volley of shots that killed him instantly. Outside, Marvin Seng heard the shots and knew that things were getting bad – *very* bad. Then he saw a familiar figure running up the track from inside the tunnel. It was Charles Johnson, the brakeman.

"What's going on?" called Charles. Then he saw the gunmen and the flaming mail car. He stopped dead. "Wha…?"

The first gunmen appeared at the door of the engine. "Let's get outta here!" he yelled. "And get rid of these guys!"

His companions didn't need to be told twice.

Without hesitating, they trained their guns on Charles and in seconds he was lying still on the ground. Next they opened fire on Marvin, who dropped to the ground like a rag doll, too. Then, leaving the mail car still blazing, the gunmen disappeared as mysteriously as they had come.

It was October 11, 1923. News of the attempted train robbery spread quickly as terrified passengers from the back of the train made their way out, past the blackened mail car and the bodies of the crew, and on to the nearest town. Before the day was out, the train was swarming with officials and policemen – representatives from the railroad police, the sheriff and his deputies, even detectives from the post office.

"Four dead," muttered the sheriff. "Sydney Bates, engineer. Edwin Daugherty, mail clerk. Marvin Seng, fireman. Charles Johnson, brakeman." He looked around at the carnage of the scene. "Who *were* these guys?"

"The mail car's burned out, sir," said one of his deputies. "Doesn't look like they took anything. Looks like they blew up the car too well, and had to make a getaway."

"You find anything?"

"Those detectives have pulled out a detonator," replied the deputy. "All we've got is this."

He held out a box which contained a sawn-off Colt revolver, a pair of greasy blue denim overalls, and some sacking shoe covers soaked in creosote.

"1 guess the shoe covers were to fool the sniffer dogs," said the sheriff, scratching his head. "Looks like they left in some kind of panic. But it doesn't look like this lot is going to help us much."

The deputy shook his head in agreement. "It's not a lot to go on. 1 think those guys might have got clean away."

Over the next few days, the police services struggled to make sense of the few, random clues. Someone suggested that the greasy overalls might have belonged to a car mechanic, and a search was carried out for suspicious characters. They found a mechanic with overalls that seemed to be covered in a similar sort of grease, and arrested him. He protested. He claimed he hadn't been anywhere near the train. Uneasily, the police realized he was probably telling the truth, but they kept him in for questioning all the same.

The investigation was going nowhere. But this was a serious crime: four murders and a whole trainful of terrified passengers. Realizing that they needed an expert eye on the evidence, the investigators decided to make a phone call to Edward Heinrich in California. The police explained the situation, and Heinrich agreed to take on the case personally.

"We can't make head nor tail of it here," the investigator told him. "We've arrested a young mechanic, but he can't have been acting on his own. There's not much against him."

"OK, send me everything you've got," said Heinrich. "I'll need every scrap of evidence that you found at the scene. Everything! Nothing's too small or unimportant. I'll take a look at it, and get back to you."

A few days later, Heinrich called the police department, as he had promised.

"You have anything for us, Dr. Heinrich?" inquired the investigator.

"I think so," said Heinrich, in his quiet, confident voice. "First of all, you should release your suspected car mechanic. The grease on these overalls does not come from cars. It's pitch, from fir trees."

"You don't say!" exclaimed the investigator. "Well, we'll release him right away."

"The man you should be looking for is a lumberjack," continued Heinrich calmly. "He is left-handed, and works mainly in the logging camps of the Pacific northwest. He is in his early twenties, about 5'10", and weighs approximately 165 pounds. He has light brown hair…"

"Hey, wait a minute," the investigator interrupted him. "We need to take all this stuff down. How in the devil's name have you worked it all out?"

"It's all very simple," said Heinrich, sounding mildly amused. "Please, allow me to finish my description of the wanted man."

"Go ahead, go ahead," said the investigator hastily.

"Well, he rolls his own cigarettes," said the

scientist. "And he is generally fussy about his appearance – much more fussy than the average lumberjack, I would say."

The investigator let out a long breath.

"That's… amazing, Dr. Heinrich," he said, in awe. "It's a great help. We'll get to work on tracking him down right away."

"Of course, I'll be happy to explain my conclusions," Heinrich told him. "All in good time. I need to finish my inspections first."

"You mean… you haven't finished yet?" gasped the police officer. "You'll be able to tell even *more*?"

"Oh yes, I should think so," Heinrich assured him. "I'll be in touch again soon."

So Dr. Heinrich went back to his meticulous examination of the evidence. He was quite sure of what he had discovered so far – and it had all come from careful, detailed examination of the overalls. He gave them a final once-over, then moved on to the shoe covers and the revolver. The next time he phoned the police department, he did indeed have more to say.

"You're looking for a man with small hands and feet. Not the greatest piece of evidence, I know," he said, with a chuckle. "But it might help. You might be rather more interested in tracking down the origin of a registered mail receipt, number 236-L. And I have a Colt serial number for you, too."

"But it was a sawn-off pistol," commented the

investigator, puzzled. "How did you get hold of the serial number?"

"My dear man," said Heinrich patiently. "You are a police officer. Surely you know that gun manufacturers stamp an additional serial number *inside* their products these days?"

"Er… no, I didn't know that," stammered the police officer. "Well, we shall follow it all up, of course."

These new leads soon had startling results. The Post Office managed to trace the mail receipt to an outlet in Eugene, Oregon. Someone named Roy D'Autremont had sent $50 to Ray D'Autremont in Lakewood, New Mexico. Records showed that Roy and Ray were twins. They also had another brother, named Hugh. Now hot on the scent, the police located their father, Paul D'Autremont, and questioned him about his sons. It soon became clear that Roy matched the description given by Heinrich - in every detail.

"So where are your sons now?" asked the police investigators.

Paul D'Autremont shrugged. "No idea where they are," he said honestly. "No one's seen them since October 11 or so."

"October 11?" asked the policeman in excitement - for October 11 was the date of the train robbery. "You sure about that?"

"Pretty sure," said Paul. "Why, I hope they ain't

been up to no mischief."

"We'll let you know, Mr. D'Autremont," the investigator assured him. "Thanks for your help."

Armed at last with some serious evidence, the police followed up the lead on the Colt pistol. It had originally been sold in Seattle, to a man named William Elliot. The dealer was helpful, and produced details of the sale – including the signature of the buyer. It was time to go back to Oscar Heinrich. Could "William Elliot" be one of the D'Autremont brothers?

Heinrich asked for a sample of the brothers' handwriting and compared it to the signature given in the gun store. Sure enough, he soon confirmed without any doubt that William Elliot and Roy D'Autremont were one and the same man.

So the police now knew *who* they were after – but *where* were they? All three men seemed to have disappeared without a trace. "Wanted" posters were issued all around the world, with a $15,000 reward for information. But nothing happened. No one seemed to have seen the men since their violent and desperately unsuccessful robbery.

The months dragged on. The investigation seemed to be getting nowhere. Meanwhile, people begged to know how Oscar Heinrich had reached his remarkable conclusions. He was only too willing to explain, and did so to an enraptured audience. He laid out the overalls before them.

"Much of my work is a simple matter of attention

to detail," he explained. "I concluded that the man was a lumberjack for two reasons. Firstly, fir pitch looks quite different from car grease under the microscope. Secondly, the right-hand pocket of the overalls contained chips of Douglas Fir, a tree that is common in the forests of the Pacific northwest."

He put his hand in one of the pockets and brought out a few tiny woodchips. "Now, I said the chips were in the *right-hand* pocket of the overalls. Think of a man cutting down a tree. He stands sideways on, with his strongest hand farthest from the trunk. It therefore follows that the flying chips of wood will land predominantly in the pockets of his weaker hand. So, you see, these overalls belong to a left-handed man."

The audience nodded, clearly impressed. "This is confirmed by the wear on the overalls – you can see that the left-handed pocket shows greater wear and tear – and suggested by the fact that the overalls button from the left," continued Heinrich.

"Now. Back to the pockets – a mine of information. As well as the woodchips, I discovered shreds of loose tobacco in both pockets. Clearly, he rolls his own cigarettes. And finally, clinging to one of the pocket seams, I discovered some very neat fingernail parings. This is a man who takes care that his hands are looking neat and tidy – not the usual concern of a lumberjack, as I think you'll agree."

The audience laughed, and Heinrich smiled at their appreciation. "So, we move on to other details –

and I emphasise the word *details*," he carried on. "My examination revealed a single strand of hair, caught by one of the buttons. It was light brown and, under the microscope, it was possible to tell that the level of pigmentation was that of a person in their early twenties. There we have the *age* of our wanted man."

"Now for the most useful piece of information of all." Heinrich held up the overalls and indicated a narrow pencil pocket on the chest area. "Inside this pocket, right at the bottom and barely in one piece, I found a tiny wad of paper. It had been washed a number of times, along with the overalls. By taking extreme care, I was able to unravel this paper and, with the help of some iodine, decipher the faded number upon it. As you are no doubt aware, that was mail receipt number 236-L, the clue that led us to our identification."

He held up the overalls for a final time. "Height and weight of our suspect - elementary; a simple matter of measuring the overalls and checking who would fit into them."

He put the overalls down and picked up the sacking shoe covers. "Not much to discover from these. But it was worth observing that they were of a small size, and that their owner would therefore have small hands as well."

Next, he picked up the Colt revolver. "Another vital clue," he said. "As everyone should now be aware, gun manufacturers stamp the inside as well as the barrel. Therefore the trick of shearing off the barrel to discard the serial number no longer works."

"And finally," he concluded, holding up two pieces of paper, "the signature of the gun's purchaser, along with a sample of our suspect's handwriting. Close examination reveals that they were written by the same hand – a Mr. Roy D'Autremont, who unfortunately is elusive, and still at large. I wish my police colleagues all the best in bringing him to justice."

The audience applauded and dispersed, but it was as Heinrich had said: there was still no sign of the brothers anywhere.

It was not until March 1927, three and a half years after the attempted robbery, that an army sergeant spotted one of the "Wanted" posters and saw a familiar face. He had served in the Philippines, and recognized Hugh D'Autremont as a private soldier who had served with him. He contacted the police, who immediately made inquiries with the Philippine authorities. Astonishingly, Hugh was found relatively quickly in the city of Manila, and placed under arrest.

A month later, the twins Ray and Roy were discovered in the town of Steubenville, Ohio, working in a steel mill under the name of Goodwin. The brothers were brought to trial, and were found guilty. All three were sentenced to life imprisonment.

## The artificial silk factory

It was 1925, two years after Edward Heinrich had impressed the world with the case of the D'Autremont brothers, and his reputation was growing. It seemed that no area of forensic science or detection was beyond him – he carried out autopsies, noticed the slightest pieces of evidence, made astonishing deductions… and he was certainly much, much smarter than a man named Charles Schwartz.

"Hi, honey, I'm home!" called Charles one day, coming through the front door. "Where are you? I've got something to show you!"

"Hi there, I'm here," sang Mrs. Schwartz, appearing in the kitchen doorway. She gave her husband a kiss and took his coat. He seemed nervous and excited all at once. "I'll just hang this up," she said. "What's the big news?"

"Come and sit down next to me," he said, heading for the couch and opening his bag. "And take a look at *this*."

Excited and curious, Mrs. Schwartz sat down next to her husband. She peered at the object he was laying out on his knees and gasped. It looked just like a piece of silk in luscious red, its texture rich and smooth.

"Why, Charles!" she exclaimed. "Did you make that in your factory?"

"I sure did," said Charles. "All my own work."

Mrs. Schwartz took a deep breath. "It's *beautiful*!" she said, her voice shaking with admiration. "It looks just like Chinese silk. Just like the real thing. You've done it at last, you clever, clever man!"

Charles nodded. "Yeah, it's a breakthrough," he said, with a broad smile. "Honey, we're going to be rich!"

Mrs. Schwartz laughed, and flung her arms around his neck. They hugged for a moment. Then Charles gently pulled back and took his wife's hands in his own. His expression was serious.

"This sure is an amazing moment for me. No one else can make artificial silk like this. You know how much work I've put into it. Long hours and a lot of money."

Mrs. Schwartz nodded. "Yes, darling, I know. Most of my savings have gone now. But it's worth it for this, isn't it?"

Charles nodded. "Yes," he said quietly. "But you must promise me something." His face darkened, and Mrs. Schwartz felt suddenly anxious.

"Of course," she whispered. "Anything. What is it?"

"We must keep quiet about it," said Charles, his voice low and urgent. "There are people out there who would do anything for a business secret like this. And I mean *anything*. Honey, if this gets out I could be in great danger."

His wife's eyes widened in fear and concern. "Danger?" she said, swallowing. "I won't breathe a word to anyone! Charles, you will be safe, won't you?"

"Yes, yes, I'll be fine," said Charles. "As long as you keep it under your hat. I'll be telling a few people, but you must leave it to me. I know who I can trust. Do you understand?"

"Oh yes," breathed Mrs. Schwartz. "I understand perfectly."

And so it was that Charles Schwartz, of Walnut Creek, California, announced casually to a few of his acquaintances that he had at last learned the secret of making artificial silk – fabric so fine that no one would ever be able to tell it apart from the real thing. The luscious piece of red silk was shown around for people to admire. So when he warned them to keep quiet about it, they didn't blame him. It was obvious that he could strike it rich with a secret like that.

Then, on the night of July 30, 1925, disaster struck. In a sudden, violent explosion, the Schwartz laboratory went up in flames. There was no hope of saving it. Within a few short hours, the place was reduced to cinders. And, when the heat had subsided, one badly charred body was pulled out of the ruins. It seemed that Charles Schwartz had met the end he feared so much...

Police investigators asked a hysterical Mrs. Schwartz to identify his body. It was a gruesome task – the body was so badly burned it was unrecognizable. But, bravely, Mrs. Schwartz peeked at a blackened wristwatch. "That was his watch," she whispered through her tears. "Yes, this is my husband."

As she was led away, one police investigator emerged from the blackened ruins shaking his head. "Definitely foul play," he said to his colleagues. "We've found detonators. Dynamite. The place was torched pretty thoroughly. I think we'd better call Heinrich."

A couple of days later, Edward Heinrich was on the job. He took a look around the burned-down building.

"Anything I should know?" he asked the police officers in charge.

"He was running some kind of laboratory, we've been told," replied the police officers. "A silk business, apparently. It's all burned out. Difficult to say what was going on, not a lot left to see."

Heinrich nodded. "Funny sort of laboratory," he commented. "I'd say there wasn't much here in the first place. I suggest you take a look at the utility bills. Anything else?"

"We've been contacted by an insurance company," said one officer. "Schwartz had life insurance amounting to $185,000, due to be paid to his wife in the event of his death. Obviously, that's a lot of money. They've asked for verification that he's actually dead."

Heinrich nodded sagely. "I don't blame them," he

said. "I'll be performing an autopsy, of course. Could you get a photograph of Schwartz from his wife, please?"

"Certainly, Dr. Heinrich," said the police officers. "We'll go over there right away."

When the police arrived, poor Mrs. Schwartz was in a terrible state. The police officers were hardly surprised – after all, she had just lost her husband. But she had more news to tell them.

"I've been robbed," she sobbed. "All my photos of Charles have gone. Every single one. I can't believe it, I really can't – after everything that's happened…"

*How extraordinary*, thought the police officers. They hadn't even mentioned what they had come for yet!

"I know it's a difficult time for you, Mrs. Schwartz," said one police officer gently. "But can you tell us if anything else was stolen? Have you noticed anything missing?"

Through her tears, Mrs. Schwartz shook her head. "Nothing else," she sniffed. "Just the photos. Why would anyone want photos of my husband?"

"Well, strange thing is, that's exactly what we've come for," explained the officer. "We need a picture of Mr. Schwartz for our investigations. Can you think of anyone who might have one?"

Mrs. Schwartz grew calmer. She dabbed at her eyes and frowned. "There is one place," she said slowly. "Charles had his photo taken by a professional not so long back. Some guy in Oakland. He might have a copy – or the negative."

"That's really helpful of you, Mrs. Schwartz," said the police officer gratefully. "We appreciate how painful this must be for you. We'll be in touch very shortly."

Meanwhile, Heinrich was taking his first look at the gruesome charred body. One fact struck him immediately. He pointed to the head and spoke to his assistant.

"The cause of death," he said, "was *not* the explosion. This man was beaten to death with a blunt instrument beforehand. And if you look closely, you'll see that the eyes were not burned out. They were gouged out. I think we need to have another little chat with Mrs. Schwartz."

Quickly, Heinrich compiled a list of questions for the grieving woman. What did Schwartz have to eat on the night of the fire? Did he have brown eyes, or blue? How tall was he supposed to be? What was his history? Had he always been an inventor?

"Ask her to provide a sample of his hair," added Heinrich, handing the list to a police officer. "There's sure to be a comb or a hairbrush in the house somewhere. Just a couple of strands will do." He paused, then added, "And I think you should carry out a check on all records relating to Mr. Charles Schwartz. The results may be surprising. You can bring his dental records directly to me."

The police came back furnished with all the

information the scientist required, including a photograph of Schwartz fresh from the photographer's studio, and a folder containing his dental records.

"Ah, thank you," said Heinrich, with a smile. "Now, I suspect that things are going to get interesting." He studied the photograph for a moment. "Just as I thought. The body I have on my autopsy slab is almost certainly *not* Charles Schwartz."

It didn't take Heinrich long to confirm his suspicions. The ears were the wrong shape, for a start, and under the microscope the hairs did not match.

"A meal of cucumber and beans?" muttered the scientist, as he examined the contents of the stomach. "Well, there's only undigested meat here."

Then he checked the dental records. "You see, this jaw appears to match the records," he pointed out to his assistant. "There is a molar missing from the right upper jaw – removed quite recently, according to his dentist." He probed the socket gently. "But not *that* recently. This socket is still raw. The molar was almost certainly removed after death."

Heinrich worked meticulously for several more hours and made further interesting discoveries. The corpse was three inches taller than Schwartz, and the charred fingertips were corroded with acid, presumably to remove the fingerprints. Someone had gone to an awful lot of trouble to disguise this corpse. And it didn't take much working out to guess who was at the bottom of it. With a $185,000 life insurance premium waiting to be picked up, it seemed very likely indeed that Charles Schwartz had staged his own death.

The police soon came up with further nuggets of information. According to Mrs. Schwartz, Charles had been a pilot in the First World War, and had studied chemistry ever since. But records suggested otherwise.

"Thing is, Dr. Heinrich," explained a detective, "Charles Schwartz was only nine years old when then war broke out."

Heinrich shook his head. "Poor, gullible Mrs. Schwartz," he said. "She's been taken in good and proper. I suppose he was spending all her money, too."

"That's right, sir," agreed the police officer. "It seems that she believed he was some kind of genius. She didn't worry about her money disappearing – she thought this silk business would make them rich."

"Ah," said Heinrich. "The silk business. Any progress on that?"

"Sure thing, Dr. Heinrich." The police officer smiled. "We checked the utility bills, as you suggested. There was nothing much happening in that laboratory. No water or gas, and just enough electricity to keep a light bulb running."

"And the silk itself?"

"We thought we'd ask you to check that, sir. But

we suspect it corresponds to one of Schwartz's cheque stubs. He bought a skein of Chinese silk from a store in San Francisco, not so long ago. Paid $8 for it."

The police officer handed Heinrich the piece of red silk. He fingered it gently. "Seems like the real thing to me," he said. "But obviously I'll make sure."

"Absolutely," agreed the police officer with a grin. "Though I don't think anyone will be surprised at what you find."

Tests soon revealed that the silk was indeed genuine Chinese silk. There was nothing artificial about it at all. Charles Schwartz's "breakthrough" was nothing more than a big scam, part of an elaborate scheme to get hold of $185,000 insurance money.

But a puzzling question remained. If it wasn't Schwartz lying on Heinrich's slab, who was it? Heinrich joined police officers searching for clues at the burned-down "silk factory", and found some charred pieces of paper – pamphlets of some kind. Heinrich took them away and examined them under the microscope. They were religious pamphlets, and Heinrich could just work out the handwritten words *G. W. Barbe* and *Amarillo, Texas* on one of them.

The police made inquiries among Schwartz's acquaintances. Yes, they were told: G.W. Barbe was a friend of Schwartz's. He was a wandering preacher who never stopped for long in one place. An ideal candidate for a mystery disappearance! Even more significantly, it was said that Barbe and Schwartz bore a strong physical resemblance to one another. There were a few crucial differences, naturally. Schwartz had brown eyes, whereas Barbe's had been a watery blue; Barbe was three inches taller; Barbe wasn't missing a molar from his upper right-hand jaw...

There seemed little doubt that Schwartz had deliberately befriended the preacher, with the idea that he would make a suitable victim. To the distraught Mrs. Schwartz, it seemed impossible that her husband could have planned such a horrendous crime so meticulously. But more evidence was yet to come. An advertisement was found among Schwartz's papers for a pharmacist's assistant. Strangely, it requested someone with small hands and feet. It was now more than obvious why: Schwartz himself had small hands and feet, and was looking for a "match". He had actually been *advertizing* for a victim when he met Barbe...

The mystery solved, all that remained was the task of actually tracking Schwartz down and arresting him. It was clear that if he was going to get his hands on the insurance money, he would have to contact his wife at some stage, for the insurance company would pay it directly to her. No doubt Schwartz believed that the sweet, gullible Mrs. Schwartz would be only too happy to know he was alive and well, and would instantly agree to run away with him.

So the police laid a trap. They encouraged

newspapers to publish the news that his wife had received the money. Meanwhile, they issued a warning to the owners of hotels and boarding houses that Schwartz might be among their guests. This warning caught the attention of a boarding house landlord in Oakland. That picture of Schwartz - didn't it look like that lodger he'd taken in recently? He checked the dates. "Mr. Harold Warren" had checked in the day after the "silk factory" had gone up in flames.

The police arrived promptly and knocked on the door of the so-called "Mr. Warren". There was no answer. Another knock, and this time they heard the sound of a single shot being fired. They decided to storm the room.

Inside, on the table, was a note addressed to Mrs. Schwartz. It was from her husband. In it, he admitted his crime, and begged for her forgiveness. And lying on the floor was Charles Schwartz himself, dead, with a smoking pistol in his hand.

He had shot himself.

# The man who was someone else

Ottilie Meissonier was well educated – she was a music teacher, and she spoke several languages. But, even so, she wasn't used to being mistaken for a lady. So when it happened it came as rather a nice surprise. She was walking along Victoria Street in London on November 26, 1895 when a man walked past her, then stopped and turned.

"Good day. It's Lady Everton, isn't it?" he said.

Ottilie spun around. There, smiling and raising his hat, stood a well-dressed gentleman, clearly much wealthier than she was herself. She guessed he was in his fifties or so.

"Oh…" she began, flustered.

But then, having seen her face, the gentleman became embarrassed. "I'm terribly sorry," he said. "I mistook you for someone else. But never mind. Where are you going? Would you care to walk a little way with me?"

Ottilie was pleased and flattered. "Well – I was just on my way to a flower show," she explained.

"Really?" responded the man. "I say, now there's a coincidence. I'm a great flower lover myself – in fact,

I employ ten gardeners on my estate in Lincolnshire. They grow the most magnificent blooms. Much finer than any you will see at the show, I can assure you."

An estate in Lincolnshire! He must be very wealthy indeed. Ottilie looked him up and down, feeling slightly awed. Could this conversation really be happening to her? They walked slowly up the road, the man chatting away easily.

"Do you have a special flower?" he asked her.

"I love chrysanthemums," Ottilie told him. "In fact, I had some delivered this morning. Very fine they are, too."

"How charming," said the man. "I love chrysanthemums, too." He stopped walking and looked at her questioningly. "Miss…?"

"Meissonier," she filled in for him.

"Miss Meissonier," he said. "Would you give me the pleasure of allowing me to visit tomorrow? I should very much like to see these fine chrysanthemums."

Ottilie was almost beside herself with astonishment. "Why… I don't live anywhere very grand," she stuttered. "I'm sure a gentleman like you…"

"Oh, don't you worry about that," he assured her smoothly, fetching out a pocket notebook and a pen. "Now, what about your address?"

Her cheeks slightly pink, Ottilie told him where she lived. He touched his hat and repeated that he would call by the next day. Then he melted away into the crowd. Ottilie wandered around the flower show in a daze. A real gentleman with an estate in Lincolnshire, offering to pay her a visit… it didn't seem possible.

But, sure enough, the next day there was a ring on the doorbell. Ottilie sent her servant Mary to open the door, and the very same gentleman stood there, as large as life. Mary showed him into the drawing room, then disappeared discreetly to make some tea.

Ottilie felt slightly nervous at first, but the stranger soon made her feel at ease. She told him about her music teaching, and which languages she spoke. He nodded and smiled, listening intently.

"Well," he said pleasantly, "once you have known me for a while you will no longer need to teach for a living. I am a cousin of Lord Salisbury, you see. I own a number of sizeable estates in London." He played with his moustache for a moment, then added almost apologetically. "I have an income of £180,000 a year."

Ottilie almost gasped, but managed to control herself. He was better connected and wealthier than she could ever have imagined!

His eyes twinkled at her surprise. "In fact," he said, "why don't you forget about your teaching right away? I am about to go on a little yachting trip on the Riviera with six of my friends. I would be delighted if you could come, too. With your musical skills and your grasp of languages, you would be most useful!"

"Oh! But I couldn't possibly," exclaimed Ottilie. "Really, it would be too much…" Then she wavered. A trip to the Riviera… she might never get such an opportunity again. "Well… perhaps I could come just for a fortnight," she said.

"Splendid!" said the man. "Now, you'll need better clothes than the ones you're wearing at the moment."

With a flourish, he took out a piece of paper and began to write a list of the lovely outfits she should buy.

"Go to Redfern's for these things," he told her. "I'll give you a cheque to cover them."

He sat narrowing his eyes and thinking carefully, jotting down more garments as he thought of them. Ottilie's eyes widened as she watched the list grow longer. "Stop, stop!" she protested. "I can't possibly accept so much…"

"It is nothing," said the man. "Just one thing – you must go to Cobb's for your riding habit."

"But I thought you said it was a yachting trip," objected Ottilie, feeling rather overwhelmed.

"Ah, yes. But I always have my own horses waiting, wherever we land," the man assured her. He fetched out another piece of paper and scribbled on it rapidly. "Here is your cheque for the dresses. It is for £40, and you can cash it at the Union Bank on St. James' Street. Now, let me see your jewels."

Ottilie held out her hands. She was wearing a

bracelet, a watch and a diamond ring. The man turned up his nose, his expression disappointed.

"We shall have to do something about this," he said, shaking his head. "Your bracelet will pass, but I would like to set two black pearls into it. Could I please take it with me? And I see that the glass in your watch is broken. I could have that mended at the same time. As for the rings... you can't possibly wear that diamond ring on my yacht. I shall have some other rings made for you. But I will need to borrow it to take the size of your finger."

For the first time, Ottilie thought that this all seemed a little odd. She was fond of her diamond ring, even if he did think it looked cheap!

"I would rather you didn't take this ring," she said. "But I'm sure I could find another for you to use as a measure."

She stood and hunted in her bureau for a cheaper ring, which she handed over.

"That's just fine," he said, reassuring her. "I shall have everything returned to you this evening by my porter. You can be sure it's him because he has only one arm."

Ottilie smiled and nodded, thinking how impressive this man was - so knowledgeable, and with so much money! In total, he stayed for almost an hour, chatting away. He told Ottilie that he owned part of the antique watch exhibition that was taking place in South Kensington, and so she showed him a small antique watch of her own.

Then, at last, he rose to his feet.

"I shall call by next Wednesday," he promised her, as he stood on her doorstep. "But you will get your jewels back this evening, along with a nice new ring."

Ottilie waved goodbye, then returned to the drawing room to catch her breath. Then she gasped. Her antique watch! She had left it sitting on the table while they chatted... and it had gone!

She began to feel cold inside. "Mary!" she called to her servant. "Go after that gentleman at once. He has taken my watch."

Mary scurried out after the man. She chased him along several streets, but then lost sight of him. She returned to her mistress empty-handed. Ottilie had the horrible, growing suspicion that she had been swindled. She threw on her coat, picked up the £40 cheque and list of dresses, and hurried outside, where she hailed a cab.

"The Union Bank, St. James' Street, please," she said, clambering in.

"Don't know of no Union Bank there," said the cabbie gruffly, whipping up his horses.

"Never mind. Just St. James' Street, then," Ottilie told him, though her heart was sinking.

The cabbie was right. There was no Union Bank on St. James' Street.

"I'll take you to the branch on Trafalgar Square," said the cabbie kindly. "They might be able to help."

But on Trafalgar Square the bank officials studied

the cheque and said that it had no value at all. They couldn't even be sure who had written it! Ottilie was furious. She had been completely taken in with the tales of grand estates and yachts and diamond rings… She wanted to kick herself. How could she have been so foolish?

Not surprisingly, the gentleman did not return the following Wednesday. But then, on December 16 – just over a fortnight after their first encounter – Ottilie was walking down Victoria Street when she spotted him, standing in a doorway. Immediately, she marched up to him. The man smiled sweetly as she approached.

"Sir, I know you!" she said.

The man's expression changed and he hurriedly crossed the road, breaking into a run. Ottilie chased after him, determined not to let him out of her sight. They both ran towards Victoria Station, where, much to her relief, Ottilie saw a policeman.

But the man approached the policeman before her.

"Please stop this woman from bothering me!" the man said. "You can see what sort of a woman she is. She won't leave me alone!"

"I beg your pardon!" cried Ottilie. She addressed the policeman. "Sir, this man has stolen two of my watches and a ring, and has forged a cheque for £40!"

The policeman looked at them both, wondering

who to believe. It didn't take him long to decide. He took the man's arm.

"I'm arresting you, mister," he said. "You're coming with me to the police station."

"But I've never seen this woman before in my life!" protested the man.

The policeman didn't believe a word of it.

At Rochester Row police station, the man gave his name as Adolf Beck. He said he lived at 139, Victoria Street – and repeated that he had never seen Ottilie Meissonier before in his life.

Ottilie made a statement about her encounter with the man, and when the police heard the details, they were not terribly surprised. There had been a rash of these crimes recently, reported by women who gave details that were remarkably similar.

The pattern was always the same. A well-dressed man approached them in the street, sometimes "mistaking" them for a lady. He would then claim to be a wealthy lord, often going by the name of Lord Wilton de Willoughby or the Earl of Wilton, and would tell them he had a large estate in Lincolnshire, or a large household in St. John's Wood – or both. He would take down their address and promise to visit.

During the visit, the pattern was also the same. He would offer the position of housekeeper, or an expensive trip. Then he would say that the woman's clothes and jewels weren't good enough, and that he would replace them. He would write out a cheque for the clothes and tell the woman to go to Redfern's or Cobb's; then he would ask for a ring to use as a measure. On a number of occasions he managed to acquire several rings or other jewels, and often stole other items, too.

Then he would disappear, never to be seen again. The cheques, of course, always turned out to be worthless.

After Beck's arrest, the police brought in a number of these women to see if they could identify him. It seemed like a foolproof way to gather evidence. None of the women knew each other; all they had to do was pick out the criminal from a row of at least eight or nine other men.

A total of eleven women identified Beck this way. The police detectives seemed confident that they had their man, and proceedings were soon under way for his trial. Then, out of the blue, something extraordinary happened.

The crimes were so striking that there had been a considerable amount of publicity about them. They jogged the memory of an anonymous stranger, who wrote to the police. He reminded them that such crimes had happened before. In 1877, a man named John Smith had gone on trial, and had been convicted for crimes so similar that they had to be by the same man.

The police looked into it. The stranger was right. John Smith's crimes had followed exactly the same pattern. He had been convicted, gone to prison, and had served a four-year sentence. After his conviction, he had never denied his crimes, though he had asked for a lighter sentence in view of his previous good record.

So – Adolf Beck must be none other than John Smith. The police were convinced of it, even though Beck himself continued to insist he was innocent.

Beck's lawyer, however, did listen. His name was Mr. Dutton.

"I've never seen any of these women in my life," Beck told him desperately. "And as for being John Smith… it's ridiculous! I wasn't even in the country in 1877. I was living in Peru, and I can prove it!"

Sure enough, there were plenty of people willing to say they had known Beck in Peru. It was all very odd, but Mr. Dutton came to a simple conclusion: Adolf Beck was telling the truth! He just looked very similar to the real criminal – and the real criminal was none other than John Smith. So, as the trial drew nearer, Dutton drew together Beck's case – that of mistaken identity.

In the meantime, the police at the Criminal Investigation Department (CID) were growing more and more confident that Beck was the criminal. His identification by eleven women seemed to provide an overwhelming case, although, in fact, it was the only evidence against him. Their search of his house had revealed nothing. All the same, they reasoned, how could eleven women be wrong? They were sure a jury would think that way, too.

What's odd is that they also agreed that John Smith and Adolf Beck must be the same man, but they failed to make any attempt to look closely into the descriptions of the two men. And, to make matters worse, they didn't allow Beck's lawyers to do so, either. When Dutton asked for the police records of John Smith, his request was flatly turned down. The CID's reasons were simple: the 1877 trial had nothing to do with the trial that was coming up. John Smith's records were "confidential and privileged".

It was so frustrating! Then, to compound the disaster, the judge at the trial seemed to think the same way. He decided that the jury should not be allowed to know anything about the 1877 trial, in case it influenced them; they had to judge this trial purely on the evidence relating to the more recent crimes.

It put Beck's lawyers in an impossible situation. Their whole arguement was based upon the idea that Smith and Beck were two different men – but, if they couldn't talk about Smith, how could they prove it?

Unfortunately, they couldn't. As woman after woman came to the stand and described the bizarre crime that she had experienced, it looked more and more likely that the jury would believe in Beck's guilt. And that was exactly what happened. He was convicted, and sentenced to seven years in prison.

From his prison cell, Beck wrote many letters to the British government, protesting that he was innocent, and explaining why he couldn't possibly have committed the crimes. The case wasn't even reviewed, though it became more and more obvious that Smith and Beck were not the same person. But at last Dutton got hold of Smith's records, which stated that his eyes were brown – whereas Beck's were blue! And there were many other differences, too.

Even the press became interested in the case, but to no effect. Beck completed more than five years of his sentence, and was at last released in January 1901.

It was March 22, 1904. Pauline Scott was wandering up Oxford Street when a well-dressed man approached her. He was charming, and she felt very flattered by his attention.

"I would be delighted to see you again," he told her, when they had chatted for a few moments. "If you would give me your address, I will call on you tomorrow."

Pauline was more than happy to oblige, and sure enough, he called by the next day. He told her that he was Lord Willoughby, and would not be able to stay long, as he had to go to the House of Lords.

"I would love to see you more often – though of course, you will need to improve your wardrobe and jewels," he told her.

He wrote out a list of dresses, then a cheque, and asked her for a ring to use as a measure. She gave him her cheapest ring, and also her watch, which needed mending. Then he said he would accompany her to lunch but, as his valet was very forgetful and had not given him any money that day, he would need some money. He took a sovereign from her purse – then changed his mind.

"You'd better get to the bank with that cheque I've given you," he told her. "Otherwise it will have shut!"

Pauline was so impressed with the situation that she completely forgot one simple fact – that banks didn't shut until 4pm. She rushed off, leaving the man behind. But it didn't take her long to realize that the cheque was worthless and that she had lost her ring, her watch and her sovereign...

So the crimes had started all over again – and, this time, the detectives at the CID had a good idea who was at the bottom of them. They soon found out that Adolf Beck dined regularly in a restaurant at 35, Oxford Street. When Pauline Scott described the crime that had taken place, this is where they sent her.

"Tell us if you spot the man who robbed you," they told her.

Although Adolf Beck was sitting there the whole time, she failed to identify him. But the police didn't give up. They were still sure that Beck was their man, so they laid another trap for him. This time, a detective walked with Pauline to Tottenham Court

Road, and made her wait on a corner, knowing that Beck would come along.

This time, she picked him out. "You are the man who took my jewels and my sovereign," she said, walking up to him.

Beck stared at her. "I've never seen you before in my life!" he retorted.

But it was no use. The detective came over, and arrested him. Beck's nightmare was happening all over again…

This time, five women testified against Beck, telling the same old story. They were all sure that he was the man who had defrauded them. Once again, the jury brought a verdict of guilty.

This time, however, the judge was uneasy. The evidence, although strong, didn't quite seem to add up. Beck continued to protest his innocence, and no concrete evidence had been found to link him to the crimes. Moreover, Beck claimed that he could not write fluently in English without a dictionary, unlike the real criminal, who wrote the lists of dresses so rapidly. So the judge delayed passing sentence, simply keeping Beck in custody.

Meanwhile, another extraordinary fact came to light: after Beck's arrests, the crimes had not stopped. John Smith (yes, he had been the criminal all along) was still up to his tricks… and at last, on July 7 1904, he was arrested. Unlike Adolf Beck, he pleaded guilty.

Beck was released, and was given a full pardon. He

was also given £5,000 in compensation for the time he had spent in prison. He spent it quickly, and died in 1909.

The case of Adolf Beck was a tragic miscarriage of justice. It showed up terrible flaws in the British justice system, and led to the introduction of the English Court of Criminal Appeal in 1907. The case also showed how flimsy people's memories can be, and how dangerous it is to base a conviction purely on the statement of a witness. Yes, Adolf Beck did look roughly like John Smith. But in many ways he was quite different – a different nationality (Beck was Norwegian, whereas Smith was German – to most of the women, the culprit was simply "foreign"), with blue eyes and different scars…

Fortunately, detective work has come a long way since then.

# Information, information, information

Thirteen women dead, all brutally murdered, and another seven seriously injured. It was a shocking total. For over five years, Yorkshire, in the north of England, had been terrorized by a man who became known as "the Yorkshire Ripper". The first attack had been in July 1975, but it was now January 1981, and the police seemed no closer to tracking down the killer. Surely, in this age of modern forensic science, it must be possible to work faster than that? But, on January 2, when the police eventually arrested a truck driver named Peter Sutcliffe, it was by little more than a lucky chance. So where had they been going wrong for so long?

Unfortunately, violent attacks on women are not unusual, and they are often carried out by someone that the victim knows. When, in July 1975, Anna Rogulskyj was attacked viciously from behind, given a massive blow to the head and left for dead, it was her boyfriend that the police had questioned first. But it soon became clear that he had nothing to do with it.

Anna Rogulskyj survived, but she could remember nothing about her attacker. He hadn't robbed her. In fact there didn't seem to be any motive for the assault at all. It was a mystery. Then, in August, a similar attack was carried out on 46-year-old Olive Smelt. She too survived, and was able to give a description of her attacker to the police. He was about 30, she said, and about 5 feet 10 inches tall. He had dark hair and possibly a beard.

Then, in October, the attacker struck again. This time, the woman didn't recover. Wilma McCann died from a huge blow to her head, made with something like a hammer. She had also been stabbed repeatedly. January 1976 came along, and with it the frenzied murder of Emily Jackson, which followed the same pattern as the other attacks. A year passed, and the police wondered if the attacks had stopped. But they hadn't. The next victim was Irene Richardson, in February 1977. By now, the police were aware that a particularly nasty killer was on the loose, and the search for him intensified.

The strange thing was, though, that there was very little forensic evidence to go on - or, for that matter, evidence of any sort. Unlike many murderers, this man never left his weapons behind. There were no fingerprints. The only shreds of information available to the police were the prints left by the wheels of his car, and the imprint of a size 7 or 8 Wellington boot.

The Wellington boot was pretty useless, as clues went. Thousands of men have feet of that size, and Wellingtons are hardly unusual. But the car wheels, at least, might offer a way forward – they were in a particular combination that could be pinned down to just a few types of cars. It wasn't much, but it was something. The police began to carry out checks on parked cars at night, secretly, in case the killer caught on and changed his wheels.

The task was hopeless. There were far too many cars of that type. The lead followed nowhere, and the police investigators tried to think of another angle. Perhaps there had been other murders in northern England by the same killer, but in a different area? If so, they might offer a clue. So the West Yorkshire police phoned the Lancashire division to see if they could help.

It turned out that there had been a similar murder in Lancashire, in November 1975. Joan Harrison had been killed with a blow to the back of the head, and had also received other injuries. In her case, there *were* further pieces of evidence. They suggested that the man had a gap between his teeth and belonged to the rare blood group B. But that was all. It was still very little to go on. The trail went cold yet again.

The nation waited tensely for the next attack. The rest of February and the month of March came and went. Nothing happened. Then, in April, the Ripper struck again: Patricia Atkinson was gruesomely killed, just like the others. Still no clues… May was quiet. But the next attack caused a wave of horror to sweep over the country, for the new victim, Jayne MacDonald, was only sixteen. WHY were the police getting nowhere?

The police were desperate. They interviewed thousands of people and took thousands of statements. But the more questions they asked, the more confusing the situation became. There simply wasn't anything clear to go on. Nothing at all.

Then, in July 1977, another of the Ripper's victims survived. Surely she could provide a description? Sadly, all the traumatized woman could remember was a blank where the man's face should have been. But there was another witness – a night watchman, who had seen a car leaving the scene of the crime. It was a Ford Corsair, white with a dark roof. A concrete clue, at last!

But it still led nowhere. During that summer, the police revealed that they had interviewed 175,000 people and taken 12,500 statements. They had also checked 10,000 cars. They appealed to the public for help – someone, somewhere must know who the Ripper was. His wife? His mother? His colleagues? The public, growing frantic, phoned and wrote in droves, and the pile of police "information" grew even higher. But it was all useless. They were no nearer to a result than they had been two years earlier.

There was a break for a couple of months, but it

seemed inevitable that the attacks would continue. Sure enough, they did. In October 1977, the body of Jean Jordan was found, and nearby lay another tantalizing clue. In her handbag, the police found a brand-new £5 note. Jean was a prostitute, and it seemed likely that the killer had given her the £5 before attacking her.

This was a valuable piece of information. Every bank note has a number, and this note was so new that it had probably gone directly from the bank into someone's account. The police immediately tried to work out which notes had gone to which companies. They soon had a list of companies that employed, between them, 8,000 men.

The police began a long, long interview process. They interviewed all the employees at a long-distance truck drivers' company called W. H. Clark (Holdings) Ltd, including a quiet truck driver named Peter Sutcliffe. But there didn't seem to be anything unusual about him, or any of the other men they questioned. They were getting nowhere.

In December 1977, another victim survived, and gave a description of the man who had attacked her. He had dark hair and a beard, she said. He was about 30, and quite stocky. He had been very friendly and relaxed and he drove a purple car. Quite a lot of evidence? Perhaps. But it still didn't seem to help. The inquiry dragged on into 1978. Three more murders took place – two in January, another in May. Nine dead; eight injured. One of the murders revealed another tiny forensic clue: traces of engineering oil were found in one of the women's wounds. Perhaps the killer worked for an engineering firm? Possibly. Possibly not.

But 1979 brought a breakthrough. Someone started writing to George Oldfield, the chief investigator in charge of the case. There were three letters, all posted in Sunderland, much further north than the area of inquiry. They were signed "Jack the Ripper", and they taunted the police for not having caught him yet. Even worse, they threatened that there were more attacks to come.

At first, it seemed probable that the letters were from a hoaxer. But when the third one arrived, it seemed to contain information that only the Ripper could have known. The police thought that at last they were on to something. They conducted forensic tests, and found traces of saliva, where the envelope had been licked. The sender belonged to the rare blood group B. Could he be the man who had attacked Joan Harrison? The police thought he must be.

And then a cassette tape arrived. No letter this time – just the tape, but the envelope was addressed in the same handwriting. The police listened to the message recorded on it. In a strongly accented voice, the man mocked the police. "You are no nearer catching me now than four years ago when I started…" he boasted. "At the rate I'm going, I should be in the book of records."

The police listened to the evil laugh at the end of the message in disbelief. This man was a monster! But surely, with his voice, his blood group and some idea of his job, they could track him down? The north of England is a region with many different dialects and accents. They are very distinctive. It was obvious that the man was a "Geordie", someone from Newcastle or the area around it. When a voice expert was called in, the location was pinpointed even further – this man, he claimed, was from the mining town of Castletown.

Hurriedly, the police investigation shifted from the area around Bradford and Leeds to Newcastle, farther north, and a massive inquiry was launched in Castletown. The police were determined to be thorough, and began to interview every single household systematically. In the late 1970s, computer systems were still unsophisticated, so they set up a massive filing system to deal with the results – boxes and boxes of little white cards... so many it was impossible to keep track of them all. The police were soon drowning in yet more information – and none of it seemed to help.

Meanwhile, the killings continued. There was Josephine Whitaker in April 1979. Then, in September, a woman named Barbara Leach. The investigation dragged on throughout the next year. Had the Ripper gone quiet? The police hoped so, but in August 1980, Marguerite Wallis met her end, too.

With each new killing, the public went into a frenzy. The police were bombarded with offers of help and thousands of pieces of information. Clairvoyants, mystics and cranks all piled in to interfere or "help" – they were sure that his name was Ronnie, or Jonnie, or maybe something else; some said he was an electrician, or perhaps a mechanic, or maybe he worked on a pumping station. In retrospect, one of the clairvoyants seems to have come quite close to the truth. Nella Jones, from London, claimed that he was named Peter and drove a truck with a "C" on its side. His house number was 6, and she even predicted the date of his next attack: November 17, 1980. On that date, the Ripper killed Jacqueline Hill, his thirteenth and final murder victim.

But how could the police evaluate this sort of information? In retrospect, it was easy to say that Nella Jones had been right, but at the time she made lots of other claims, too – many of which did not turn out to be accurate at all. Picking out the bits that might be true was an impossible task. It was the same with the story of the entire case: too much useless information, information, information…

Tired, despondent, despairing, the police kept on plodding. They went back to the £5 note clue, and conducted more interviews. They looked for owners of white Ford Corsairs. They checked on engineering firms, or firms that had anything to do with engineering. Time and time again, they returned to W.H. Clark, the truck driving firm. Peter Sutcliffe was interviewed as many as nine times, but he was quiet and well-behaved – a perfect employee. He had a quiet wife, who could always say where he had been late at night.

Anyway, in most people's minds, the Yorkshire Ripper was a Geordie. The chief investigator thought so. Most of the public thought so. Many police officers thought so. But the investigation was so vast, that one vital fact had been overlooked.

The letters and the tape recorded in a Geordie accent had been linked to the Ripper because they contained details about one of the victims. But what the police failed to realize was how many details were *out there* – in newspapers, on the street, everywhere. *Anyone* could have picked up this "inside information". In fact, there was nothing to link the letters to the Ripper at all – only the desperate belief of police officers who had very little else to go on…

The real Ripper didn't have a Geordie accent, nor did he come from Newcastle. Peter Sutcliffe was leading a very quiet and "normal" life in Bradford – with a Bradford accent. The whole time.

After five gruesome years, the huge, grinding investigation still wasn't homing in on the Ripper. In fact, in January 1981, it was the Ripper himself who made a mistake. And it wasn't quite the mistake that the police might have expected.

On January 2, two police officers were out on a routine patrol in the town of Sheffield when they spotted a car with a man and woman inside. It was an area known for prostitution, which is illegal; so the police wandered over to check on who the couple might be.

The man inside the car had a dark hair and a beard, and was aged about 30.

"Your name, please, sir?" P. C. Hydes asked him.

"Peter Williams," answered the man. He seemed nervous. "This is my girlfriend," he added.

The officers knew the area well, and Sergeant Ring recognized the woman. He was quite sure she wasn't the man's "girlfriend". She'd been in trouble with the police before. "You'd better come with us," he said to her, and she clambered out of the car.

The man got out of the car too. "I've just got to go to the toilet," he told the police officers, as they escorted the woman away. Hurriedly, he disappeared around the back of a nearby industrial building.

When he came back, the police officers were taking a closer look at his car. It was a Rover, or so it seemed. They took a note of the plate, and phoned the central information bureau to check the registration number.

Surprise, surprise! Its plate didn't belong to a Rover at all. It belonged to a Skoda. The officers checked with the bureau again. Definitely a Skoda! And the Rover belonged not to Peter Williams, but to Peter Sutcliffe, who lived at 6, Garden Lane, Heaton, Bradford. They bent down and inspected the number again - and discovered that it was taped on with black tape, over the top of the original.

"A false plate? You'd better come with us, sir," said Sergeant Ring.

And that was the beginning of the end for Peter Sutcliffe - at long last.

In the police station, Peter Sutcliffe seemed very calm. He asked to go to the toilet, then answered any questions the police asked him. After all, being in possession of false plates was not a major crime.

But the police were not going to let him go without some careful questioning. He matched the description given by some of the Ripper's victims. He had size 7 feet. He belonged to the rare blood group B. He had a gap between his teeth. He seemed to own a number of cars. He had been interviewed several times at W.H. Clark Ltd. There was a question mark hanging over him. For the time being, the police kept him in.

It was not until the next day that a bell began to tinkle in the mind of Sergeant Ring. That man he'd arrested the night before - there was something funny about him. All police officers were on high alert for anyone who might be the Ripper. What if this was their man? Wasn't it a little bit strange that he had disappeared around the back of a dark building like that, just when the police had arrived?

Without telling anyone where he was going, Sergeant Ring returned to the scene of the arrest. He retraced Peter Sutcliffe's footsteps around the side of the dark building. And there, placed carefully behind a storage tank, was a hammer, and a knife.

Sergeant Ring was jubilant. He had found the vital clue! He rushed to the police station to inform his colleagues. It now seemed certain that they'd found the Ripper – even if it was by accident.

Officers began to question Sutcliffe again, without revealing their suspicions. They questioned his wife again, and checked her alibis. One of them didn't match, and the police probed Sutcliffe more closely. After a while, they mentioned the hammer and the knife, too. Sutcliffe was being driven slowly, surely, into a corner... and at last, he broke down.

"I think you are leading up to the Yorkshire Ripper," he said suddenly.

"What about the Yorkshire Ripper?" asked one of the officers.

"Well," said Peter Sutcliffe. "That's me."

Once he had made the confession, Sutcliffe proceeded to tell the police the whole gory story of his murderous life over the previous five years. He also revealed that he had hidden another knife in a toilet cistern at the police station, shortly after being arrested. The only murder he had *not* committed was that of Joan Harrison – the one that had yielded the clue about his rare blood group, and the gap between his teeth. By a strange coincidence, both these clues pointed to Sutcliffe. It was the only lucky break in a case that had taken far too long to solve.

On May 22, 1981, Peter Sutcliffe was found guilty of thirteen murders, and was sentenced to life imprisonment. He is still in prison to this day.

# The doctor's secret

On a wind-blasted, stormy night in August 1998, the people who lived next to Hyde cemetery got the fright of their lives. A small, quiet town near Manchester, in the north of England, was not the kind of place you'd expect to find grave-robbers or body-snatchers. But a caretaker at the retirement home overlooking the cemetery saw something that made his blood run cold.

"There are people with shovels in the graveyard," he whispered into his telephone, "and they're digging around the tombs. Send for the police."

He almost dropped the receiver when he heard the reply: "But that is the police, sir."

Detective Inspector Stan Egerton was waiting at the edge of an open grave, hoping for all the world he wasn't making a terrible mistake. He was investigating a local doctor, and had ordered forensic tests on the body of one of the doctor's former patients. Opening her coffin was a drastic step to take. But, if the doctor had a secret, Egerton was determined to find out what it was, even if it meant waking up the dead.

Dr Harold Shipman was not your average family doctor. Dr Shipman cared. His patients adored him. Bearded and bespectacled, he was fifty-one and had his own private surgery. He'd worked with other medics in the past but he preferred working alone. As he was the only doctor at the surgery, his patients always had a long wait to see him, but nobody minded. Everyone knew that when their turn came, Shipman would give them his special attention. He listened to his patients' problems, their family news, their hopes for the future. Like an old-fashioned practitioner, he was generous with his time.

The patients who cherished him most were the elderly women who made up a good part of his practice. They loved his cheeky jokes, which he kept up even inside his office; on his desk, he had a sign that declared Remember - Every Day's a Bonus.

One time, Shipman noticed an old lady sitting in his waiting room.

"Not you again," he said with a chuckle. "You're in here every week. It's about time we got you to sponsor that chair."

The patient in question thought this was so amusing she donated fifty pounds to the surgery fund, then and there.

And so, overall, Shipman's life looked rosy. He was happily married and lived in a large suburban house with his wife, Primrose, their daughter and three sons. He worked for local charities, supported his son's rugby team and was interested in new technology, computers in particular (in fact, he considered himself something of a computer expert). If ever there was a picture of a successful family doctor, Harold Shipman was it.

The surgery was as busy as ever on the morning Angela Woodruff arrived. She got straight to the point.

"Dr Shipman, I want to know exactly how my mother died."

"Oh yes," he replied. "You're Kathleen Grundy's daughter. Your mother's death was unexpected, wasn't it?"

Unexpected was the right word, thought Angela Grundy. Her mother might have been coming up for her eighty-second birthday, but she lived life to the full. She loved walking and taking holidays, she worked part-time for local charities and was in great physical condition. Her friends couldn't believe she had died so suddenly. Only the day before her death, she had been out walking and had popped into the bank to deposit some money. Kathleen was quite a rich woman.

"So, could you tell me what happened?" Angela asked the doctor.

Shipman explained that two of Mrs Grundy's friends had called him out. When Kathleen had failed to turn up at a charity lunch, they had gone to see if she was in any trouble. There was no answer to their frantic knocking, but the front door of her cottage was unlocked, so they went inside and found Kathleen stretched out on a sofa. She had been dead for an hour or more.

"Your mother died of natural causes," said Shipman confidently. "I saw her earlier in the day, but only for a chat. She told me she hadn't been feeling well."

"And what did you write on her death certificate?" Angela asked.

"Old age, of course," he snapped, as if he considered it rude to question a doctor.

As she left the surgery, Angela Woodruff was feeling uneasy about Harold Shipman. She was a lawyer by profession, and 'old age' struck her as a bit vague as a cause of death. She also found him arrogant and cocky, with an oddly superior tone. Surely these weren't the qualities of a caring doctor? But Angela was so preoccupied with organizing her mother's burial that she put these doubts to the back of her mind.

At the funeral, hundreds of people came to Hyde cemetery to pay their respects. When it was over, Angela Woodruff longed to get on with her life. But then, twelve days later, she got a bewildering phone call.

"Did you know that your mother had changed her will?" a voice asked her. "She's left everything to some man called Shipman."

"That's impossible," cried Angela. "She never

mentioned it to me."

"You'd better come and see for yourself," said the stranger.

"I will," she answered. "And I think I'll bring the police along with me."

The mood at Hamilton Ward Lawyers the next morning was sombre. On the day that Kathleen had died, they had received a scruffy package in the post. It contained a letter and a 'do-it-yourself' will. The will promised Kathleen Grundy's estate (worth about £400,000) to Harold Shipman. There was not a penny for Angela or the rest of the family. Then, four days after the arrival of the first package, they had received another letter with news of Kathleen's death. It claimed to be from her friend 'J Smith', asking them to activate the will. The lawyers at Hamilton Ward thought this was all rather fishy, and were more than willing to let the police take a look.

The policeman and Angela went over the documents. It didn't take long to work out that they were forgeries. First, the papers were sloppily typed and the ink was faded. Kathleen had worked as an office secretary, and would never have passed such lazy typing. Then there was the fact that the will only mentioned one house. Kathleen owned another home, a cottage in the Lake District, but only her family and her closest friends knew about it. Last but not least, there was this mysterious 'J Smith'. John Smith is the most common false name used by criminals. It was almost laughable!

Under a microscope, the policeman could see that all three documents had been composed on the same typewriter. Two witnesses had signed the will. The police decided it was time to pay them a visit.

The witnesses soon provided another black mark against the doctor. When Shipman had asked two of his patients to sign a form for him, Paul Spencer and Claire Hamilton were happy to oblige. They didn't think of asking what it was they were signing – after all, they trusted their doctor with their lives. When the police showed them the will they were shocked. Their signatures had been copied, but were clearly clumsy forgeries. If only the police could get a recent sample of Kathleen's signature, they'd be able to compare it with the one on the will.

Angela Woodruff had the answer. She wasn't a lawyer for nothing. She dashed to her mother's bank and got a copy of the last deposit slip Kathleen had signed. Sure enough, the signature on the will was different from the one on the slip, proving that the will was a fake. Someone was trying to defraud her of almost half a million pounds! And Harold Shipman, the perfect family doctor, was the prime suspect.

The fraud case was passed to Stan Egerton, a seasoned policeman with thirty years' experience of tackling criminals. He also had an amazing memory for names and faces, and he remembered the name

"Shipman". Hadn't there been an undercover investigation into that man, only a few months earlier? He sent for the detective who'd been in charge.

"Oh, it all came to nothing," the man told him. "We had to drop it due to lack of evidence."

"But what was it about?" Egerton pressed him.

"Someone got the crazy idea that too many of his patients were dying."

Egerton suddenly remembered that Kathleen Woodruff's death was unexpected. She had years still ahead of her, according to all her friends.

"Is something wrong?" asked the other detective, seeing his expression.

"I'm not sure," answered Egerton slowly. "But we're going to have to look a little deeper into all this."

He reached for his phone. "Get me the coroner's office," he said firmly. "I need to open a grave."

The morning after the ghoulish scenes in the cemetery, the police decided to arrest Shipman right away, to prevent him from tampering with valuable evidence. They raided his office and seized the computer the doctor used to store his patients' notes. Shipman had read their search warrant and knew they were looking for a typewriter, so he fetched a portable machine from a cupboard.

"Mrs Grundy borrowed it from time to time,"

he said, bold as brass.

Once Shipman was arrested, his fingerprints were taken. The police rushed the typewriter to their laboratory and dusted it for prints. Shipman's were all over it, but there were none that matched Mrs Grundy's. Then, when the police dusted the phoney will, they found a print of Shipman's left-hand little finger, too. The forensic evidence was building up. And then the police arrived at the doctor's house.

From the outside, the Shipman family home was an unexceptional four-bedroom 'semi' on a quiet cul-de-sac. The garden was a bit messy but the house looked neat and tidy. Inside it was another story. When the police forced their way in, they had to cover their noses against the stench. It was a tip. There were piles of dirty clothes and rotting garbage stacked everywhere. The floor was so filthy the soles of the policemen's shoes stuck to the carpet. The kitchen was a no-go area. This health-hazard house certainly didn't match the doctor's squeaky-clean reputation.

The police soon found a large stash of women's jewels. None of it was particularly valuable, but it made them curious. Primrose Shipman refused to say anything, but they could tell it wasn't hers. Primrose was a large woman. There were hundreds of rings, but none of them would have fitted on her chubby fingers. So whose rings were they?

The detectives also found a hidden store of drugs. One of the drugs was morphine, a powerful painkiller. Unusually for a doctor, Shipman had no licence to keep drugs at his home; even if he had, they should have been locked in a secure container. So what was the doctor up to?

Shipman was allowed bail and Hyde buzzed with whispers. But the doctor's patients rallied around him. Hundreds of cards arrived at the surgery and the faithful reception staff stuck every one of them up in the front window. "We trust you, Harold," said one. "Hands off our doctor," demanded another. Egerton wondered if he was chasing the wrong man. But, if that was true, why was there morphine at his house?

At last, a poisons expert gave the police the answer they were looking for. She had studied samples of Kathleen Grundy's body tissue, carefully removed from the grave. The cause of death wasn't old age - it was morphine poisoning.

The police had been lucky. Morphine never breaks down and disappears, as long as the body survives. In some places, such as South America, traces of the drug have been found in the tissue of mummified bodies, dating back thousands of years. The police took Shipman in for questioning and asked him to explain how his 81-year-old patient could have died of a drug 'overdose'.

Shipman sneered. "She was an addict, of course," he answered, as though he thought the detectives were stupid. "Look at my notes," he went on. "It's all in there. See for yourselves."

Sure enough, there were computer entries about Kathleen taking drugs. "Denies everything, should I do a blood test?" was one remark, from some years before. Another said, "Could she be an addict, at her age?"

But the sneaky doctor wasn't as clever as he thought he was. His software, MicroDoc, was state of the art. Shipman had even been on the software designers' advisory panel. But what he never guessed was that on his computer's hard drive, MicroDoc made a copy of everything he did. It recorded the date and time of any changes that were made to a document. The police were able to see that Shipman had entered the comments about her drug habit after Kathleen's murder.

Shipman's credit card bill provided more evidence. On one of the days when he claimed to have been treating Kathleen, Shipman had been out shopping in a town over a hundred miles away from Hyde. There were no records of Kathleen's appointment in the surgery diary, and when they interviewed the doctor's staff, the police learned that Shipman hadn't seen any patients that day.

Upon being challenged with the evidence, the confident doctor fell to the floor and cried like a baby. For ten minutes he was trembling and muttering, on the point of confessing. But then he climbed back into his chair and refused to say another word.

While Shipman was sitting tight-lipped in the interview room, there was a knock on Egerton's door.

John Shaw was a taxi driver in Hyde. Like the doctor, he specialized in looking after the elderly, particularly women. John would pick them up and help with their shopping and other chores.

"I wasn't going to say anything," he started. "I didn't think anyone would believe me. But I've noticed that a lot of Shipman's patients have been dying."

"How many?" asked Egerton.

"At least 20. Maybe more."

Stan Egerton shook his head in disbelief. "When did all this start?"

"Years ago," came the answer.

Now the police investigation would have to look at all Shipman's ex-patients. In his time as a family doctor, Shipman had written over 500 death certificates. That was ten times the number an average family doctor would write. Slowly, methodically, the police discovered the truth.

Shipman was a serial killer, preying on his own patients. He had a well-rehearsed killing routine. The doctor arrived at his victim's house with a syringe full of deadly morphine in his pocket, and persuaded them to have an injection. Of course, they trusted him completely. But within seconds, they were dead.

Shipman made his exit and waited for the death to be reported. Then he rushed back to the house, soothed the relatives or friends of the deceased and told them he would "take care of all the details". He announced there was no need for a post-mortem (which would have exposed him as a murderer) since he knew the cause of death. He promised to write out a death certificate and advised the family to have the body cremated, hoping to destroy the morphine evidence against him, for ever.

The police now believe Harold Shipman murdered an incredible 234 of his patients this way. It seems odd that no one challenged him sooner. Five of his patients even died inside his own surgery. But everyone assumed that, because Shipman had a lot of elderly patients, he could expect to find a lot of deaths. People trust their doctor.

Throughout his gruelling trial, Shipman never confessed. When he was found guilty, the judge told him he would spend the rest of his life in jail. The doctor just shrugged his shoulders and left the court without even a glance at his wife or family. The police searched for the motive behind these staggering crimes. What had driven this ordinary, family man to become the worst serial killer in British history?

When Shipman was seventeen, his mother died of lung cancer. There was no treatment for the disease and the only thing that relieved her agonizing pain was a daily morphine injection. Each time he sat with his mother for the injection he saw the pain disappear, replaced by a smile. Perhaps he imagined his patients wanted the same 'escape' from pain, even though most of them were perfectly healthy? Or perhaps he simply enjoyed having the power of life or death over them?

During his mother's illness, Shipman became fascinated with painkillers. When he was training as a medic he started using them, and he was soon hooked. Twenty years before his arrest in Hyde, a chemist exposed Shipman as a drug addict. He went into rehab, and the General Medical Council (the board that controls doctors) decided to give him a second chance. He was fined and forbidden to keep drugs in his house. But, by forging prescriptions, he was able to stockpile morphine for use as poison.

The first time he killed, it might have been an accident. But it was enough to whet his appetite. So he began looking for victims whose deaths wouldn't surprise their relatives. The doctor thought he was better than other people. When he worked with other doctors he was always arguing with them, and if a patient dared to question him he would give them a verbal lashing. The murders made him feel all-powerful. He could decide if a patient was to live or die, and it thrilled him.

Shipman didn't usually murder for money, as he appeared to have done in the case of Kathleen

Grundy. On the rare occasions that he took something, it tended to be some kind of 'trophy'. One man, who'd just been told his mother had died, found Shipman clutching her sewing machine.

"Oh, she promised it to my wife," the doctor explained. "You don't mind, do you?"

The man was so shocked by his mother's death he didn't think of protesting. Shipman kept these reminders of his murders, hidden away among all the junk in his revolting house. But, by the time he forged Kathleen Grundy's will, the doctor had lost all sense of reality. Either he had become so demented he didn't think the police would ever catch him, or he was exhausted with the killing, to the point that he wanted to be caught. The will was so obviously a fake that it was practically an invitation to the police to arrest him.

For twenty years, Dr. Harold Shipman dispensed death. The secrets of Hyde cemetery are out in the open now. But, because of his refusal to admit his guilt, hundreds of people will never know for sure if their relatives died of natural causes, or from his deadly touch – and, for them, this is the most terrible secret of all.

# Ransom

At the offices of *Il Messaggero*, one of Rome's biggest daily newspapers, the editor's secretary was opening the mail. Among all the letters and neat-looking packages, there was one that looked slightly different from the others. The secretary was curious. She reached for it and gave it a squeeze. It seemed to contain something soft. She opened it carefully.

Inside the package was a letter, and a sealed plastic bag. The secretary pulled out the bag and held it up to see what was inside.

She stared at it. Her knees turned to jelly. And then she fainted.

Ten minutes later, the editor made a phone call.

"*Signora* Getty, this is *Il Messaggero*," he said. "The package has arrived. Can you come and identify it?"

"Yes, I'll come right away," said Gail Getty in a brave voice.

Hurriedly, she took her coat and made her way across Rome to the newspaper's buildings. There, she was ushered inside and taken to the editor's office.

"The package is here," said the editor. "It is not a

pretty sight. Take a deep breath before you look at it."

Trembling, Gail Getty leaned forward and peered at the gruesome object in the plastic bag. She felt her stomach churn. This was unbearable… she felt a wave of rage and disgust wash over her. But then she drew on every scrap of strength she had, and examined the bag closely. She nodded.

"Yes," she whispered. "That belongs to Paul."

"Are you sure, *signora*?" queried the journalist.

Gail swallowed. "Yes. That's his," she said, quietly but firmly. "It's the right shape, and those are his freckles." She looked up at the editor, her face pale. "I'm absolutely sure. This belongs to my son. It is definitely Paul's right ear."

The news reverberated around the building, then out into the streets and beyond. The kidnappers had cut off an ear! It was November 10, 1973 - exactly four months since Jean Paul Getty III had disappeared without trace from the streets of Rome.

At the time of the kidnapping, no one had been very surprised at Paul's disappearance. The sixteen-year-old grandson of Jean Paul Getty, the world's richest man, was a rebel who liked the high life. He didn't go to school and behaved exactly as he pleased - riding motorcycles, painting a few pictures and hanging around late at night with the hippy community in Rome. In the press, he was known as "the Golden Hippy", with his long red hair and Bohemian lifestyle. So when, on July 10, he didn't return home from a night out on the town, his roommates didn't think anything of it.

It was only later that day that his friend Martine began to worry. Paul *did* like to stay out late, but staying out this long was unusual.

The phone rang, and Martine picked it up.

"Hi there," said a cheerful voice. "Is Paul around?" It was Gail, Paul's mother. While Paul had a free and easy lifestyle, his mother tried to keep as close an eye on him as she could, and she often called his apartment.

"Paul's not here," said Martine. "It's a little bit strange. He didn't come back last night."

"Really?" said Gail. "That's funny." She tried to dismiss the fear that sprang up in the back of her mind. "Well, we both know Paul. I'm sure he'll be back soon. Can you ask him to call me when he shows up?"

"Of course," said Martine, and put the phone down.

Gail tried not to worry. Her son was well known for his riotous ways. He was probably just partying somewhere with his hippy friends. Even so, he usually told either her or Martine where he was…

She tried not to let her thoughts run away with her, and waited patiently. Later that night, her phone rang, and she leaped to answer it.

"Hello?" said a gruff male voice. "Is that Signora Getty?"

"Yes," Gail replied, her heart pounding. "What can

I do for you?"

"We have your son, Paul Getty," said the voice. "We have kidnapped him. We will be asking you for a lot of money to get him back."

"But I don't have any money!" protested Gail.

"Paul's grandfather does, and you know it. Please do as you're told and get what we want. If you do, your son won't come to any harm."

"But…" Gail's mouth went dry and she trailed off, feeling speechless with fear.

"You'll be hearing from us," said the sinister voice.

The line went dead. Gail gasped, then collapsed in shock.

When she came round, Gail immediately phoned the Italian police, the *Carabinieri*. Before long, a group of officers arrived at her apartment to question her. In despair, she quickly realized that they had little patience either with her or her son. Paul was notorious across Rome for his reckless lifestyle. Everyone knew about his grandfather's extraordinary wealth, but it was also common knowledge that Paul himself had little access to it. Even if he *had* been kidnapped – and the Carabinieri clearly didn't believe he had – it seemed quite likely that he'd staged the stunt himself, to get his hands on some of his grandfather's money.

That was how the newspapers saw the situation, too. Gail had no idea how they found out about Paul's disappearance, but nevertheless they had plenty to say about it the next day. "*Joke or Kidnap?*" ran the headlines. It was a nightmare.

Whatever the truth of the matter, Gail heard nothing for over a week. She was becoming frantic with worry, and the police were still doing little to help. It was almost a relief when a letter arrived from the kidnappers, although when she read what they wanted, she almost fainted all over again.

The letter demanded ten billion lire. It was an absurd amount – about $17 million! It was obvious that only one man could meet a demand like that. Gail herself could not, and neither could Paul's father, her ex-husband Jean Paul Getty II. The head of the family, Jean Paul Getty, the richest man in the world and also one of the meanest, would have to pay up to help his grandson.

In 1973, Jean Paul Getty was 79 years old. He was American, but in his later years he preferred to live in England, in a lavish mansion named Sutton Place. He was a strange man, deeply suspicious of the outside world. He had four grown sons, including Jean Paul Getty II, but he had never been a loving father. Family relationships within the Getty family were generally unhappy ones.

So, when he received news of his grandson's kidnap, Jean Paul Getty's response was perhaps predictable. He issued a statement.

"I don't believe in paying kidnappers," he announced. "I have fourteen other grandchildren, and if I pay one penny now, then I will have fourteen kidnapped grandchildren."

It is also clear that he, too, suspected Paul of trying to trick him out of the money. Gail was growing desperate.

The fact was that she had every reason to be worried. Paul's kidnapping was completely genuine. On the night of July 9, he had been wandering around the streets of Rome at about 3am, rather drunk, when a white car had pulled up beside him.

"Are you Paul Getty?" a man had asked him.

"Yes," he'd replied – and that was that. Three men bundled him into the car, and drove off at high speed. A cloth soaked in chloroform was clamped over his face and he lost consciousness as the car sped on through the night.

He came round to find that he had been tied up and had a blindfold over his eyes. The car was still going, and kept going for several hours yet. Paul lay in the back of the car in terror, wondering what was happening to him. Were they going to kill him? Would he ever see Rome and all his friends again?

At last the car stopped, and Paul was pulled out of the car feet-first. He noticed that the air was warmer, and guessed that they had driven south. It made sense – his kidnappers' accents were those of southern Italy. In fact, he was in Calabria, a remote region in the "toe" of Italy.

For the next few weeks, Paul was kept in chains in

the mountains. When his captors grew nervous, they made him move, marching him along narrow tracks to new, primitive hideouts. He was given a little food, water, and sometimes alcohol; the kidnappers also gave him a radio, on which he could listen to the news. To his horror, he realized that many people were not taking his kidnapping seriously. He was very, very frightened, but for the time being, his captors did nothing to harm him.

After a couple of weeks, the kidnappers gave Paul a piece of paper and a pen.

"We want you to write to your mother," they told him.

With his hand trembling, Paul wrote down what they instructed him to say.

"*Don't let me be killed,*" he wrote. "*Don't publicize my kidnapping… Pay, I beg you, pay up as soon as possible… This is all you have to know. If you delay, it is very dangerous for me. I love you. Paul.*"

Gail did not need further convincing that the kidnapping was genuine. But getting the police or the Getty family to take the affair seriously was still proving almost impossible. Her ex-husband, Jean Paul Getty II, didn't want to face up to the problem, and didn't want to put pressure on his father. Time drifted on, and she received another phone call from the man who had contacted her before, who gave himself the nick-name "Cinquanta". He belonged to a small group of Mafia families based in rugged, impoverished Calabria.

"Why don't you give us the money?" he demanded. "Don't you care about your son?"

"I've told you – I don't have that sort of money," insisted Gail.

"But the grandfather! Get it from him!" shouted Cinquanta.

"He won't give it to me," Gail told him.

Cinquanta found this incredible – a grandfather who would not pay to rescue his grandson! And, although Gail loathed what the kidnappers were doing, she had to agree with him. All she wanted was to get her son back – but she really, truly did not have $17 million to part with.

However, while Jean Paul Getty still refused to surrender any money, the pressure was mounting upon him to act. Given that the Italian police were getting nowhere, he sent one of his own men to look into the situation – an ex-CIA spy named J. Fletcher Chace. He arrived in Rome on August 15.

At first, Gail was relieved that someone with so much experience had arrived to help. Unfortunately, it soon became obvious that Chace had no idea how to deal with the Mafia. He didn't speak Italian, so he was useless as a negotiator; and, shortly after arriving, he was fooled into parting with $3,000 by a young man who claimed to know the kidnappers – then promptly disappeared.

What was worse, Chace seemed set on proving his employer's theory to be correct: that Paul had staged the whole thing himself to get at his grandfather's money. The situation wasn't helped when another family employee came forward and said that he had spotted Paul personally on a piazza in Rome. Chace's report back to Jean Paul made the old man more determined than ever – he wasn't going to part with a penny!

Realizing that Chace was a very poor ally, Gail decided to take matters into her own hands. August had flown by; Paul had now been missing for over six weeks. With Chace's agreement, she flew to England, in the hope that she could persuade the old man to pay up in person.

It was a futile move. Knowing what she wanted, Jean Paul refused to meet her, and still insisted on communicating only through Chace. After ten days, she gave up, and returned to Rome.

The kidnappers were getting more and more frustrated with the delays. Almost three months had gone by and the Gettys seemed no closer to paying any money. The Calabrians began to threaten that Paul would suffer if they delayed much longer.

Feeling powerless and caught in the middle between the kidnappers and the Getty family, Gail decided to take a risk. When the kidnappers invited her to meet them, she decided she had nothing to lose. They were offering her the chance to see Paul, and to negotiate face to face. Surely something positive would come out of it?

"I'll come," she told them. "Just tell me where to meet you."

So the kidnappers gave her detailed instructions for a time and place. "We shall meet you south of Naples," Cinquanta told her. "From there, we shall take you to see your son. You need have no fears for your own safety, signora."

"Thank you. I'll be there," she promised.

But, shortly after coming off the phone, she mentioned the idea to Crace. He was appalled.

"Meet these people!" he exclaimed. "Gail, you must be crazy. You can't take a risk like that. You don't know who they are, or what they might do to you."

"But I've said I'll go," protested Gail. "It might be our only chance of getting through to them."

Crace shook his head adamantly. He wouldn't hear of it. "I absolutely forbid you to go," he said firmly.

It wasn't for Crace to say what Gail should do, but nevertheless her heart sank. She knew it would only add to their fury if she failed to turn up, and she had no means of letting them know that she wasn't going. But perhaps Crace was right – perhaps it was foolish to take such a risk? She decided to follow his advice, and miss the appointment.

She later realized it had been a mistake. The kidnappers, already bursting with impatience, were furious with this latest refusal to cooperate. They decided it was time to take drastic action.

By mid–October, three months after his

kidnapping, Paul was living in a cave high in the Calabrian mountains. It was cramped and miserable, and he only had a rough foam mattress to sleep on. He was beginning to lose all sense of time, so he tried to keep track of it by making a scratch on the rocks every day. But at least his captors had still done nothing to harm him.

Then, one morning, a group of men arrived at the cave and sat down next to him. One of them produced a pair of scissors.

"We are going to cut your hair," they told him. "It's very dirty now. We have to cut it off."

Paul quickly put a hand up to his long red hair. "No!" he exclaimed. "I like it long. It's always been long."

"Tough," said the men. "We are cutting it."

Paul knew it was useless to resist, so he sat quietly as one of the men chopped off his beloved tresses, cutting them particularly short around his ears and the back of his neck. When he had finished, the man reached for a bottle of alcohol and dabbed the exposed skin behind Paul's ears.

It was then that he realized what they were going to do. Sick fear and desperation spread through his body, knowing that he was totally helpless. As one of the men blindfolded him, he sat limply, waiting for the inevitable.

"Bite on this," someone said, shoving a handkerchief into his mouth.

Then Paul felt a piercing pain as another man

grabbed his right ear and cut it off with a single stroke.

On October 21, the kidnappers told Gail what they had done. "We shall send the ear in the mail," they told her. "Then you will know that we mean business."

They were becoming more and more threatening, but the ear hadn't arrived and so Gail had no way of knowing if they had really carried out the gruesome deed. Then a newspaper received a tip-off that there was something interesting at a spot on the Rome-Naples highway. This turned out to be Polaroid photographs of Paul, with a dazed expression on his face - and missing his right ear.

Gail was horrified and sickened by the pictures, but there was still no sign of the actual ear. In fact, the postal services were extremely poor in southern Italy, and the package was delayed for a couple of weeks. It was only when it eventually arrived on November 10 that the world sat up and began to realize that perhaps, after all, young Paul Getty's life was in serious danger.

The world press began to have a field day, publishing blown-up pictures of Paul's ear. Amidst all the publicity, Jean Paul Getty began to realize that he would have to act. Thanks to the intervention of an ex-FBI agent, Thomas Biamonte, who spoke Calabrian and negotiated directly with the kidnappers, the ransom demand was lowered to

1,700 million lira (about $3.2 million). At last, in early December, Jean Paul Getty agreed to pay, and Chace was given the authority to take the money out of a bank in Rome.

On December 12, Chace delivered the money personally, along the highway from Rome to Calabria. At a signal from the kidnappers, he stopped the car and left three bags of lira notes by the side of the road. From a safe distance, police agents watched as the kidnappers picked up the bags. They managed to scribble down the registration number of their car, and followed it up later.

Shortly afterwards, the kidnappers told Paul that they had received the money at last. He was taken to a car and driven away from the mountains that had been his prison for four long months. He was dumped, blindfolded, by the side of the road.

The car drove off, and Paul was left alone. It was dark, and raining, but there was no other sound. Could he really be free at last? Cautiously, he removed his blindfold and looked around. The road was empty. Uncertain what to do, Paul set off along the road, hoping to get a lift from a passing car. Eventually, he was picked up by the local police. As Paul saw them approach, he realized his ordeal was finally over.

"I'm Paul Getty," he told them. "I want a cigarette. Look, they cut off my ear."

It seems astonishing that more was not done to

save Paul from his plight, either by his family or by the Italian police. The fact is, however, that the police still doubted the reality of his situation, right up until the moment his ear arrived in the mail. So they did little to try to locate him. Kidnappings by the Italian Mafia were on the increase in the 1970s, and the general expectation was that a wealthy family would simply pay the ransom rather than expect the police to take serious action.

Once Paul was free, however, the police did a reasonable job of identifying his captors. They managed to trace the car that had collected the ransom, and found the man who had picked up the bags. Further investigations led to the arrest of two more members of the Calabrian Mafia. Nevertheless, only $17,000 of the ransom money was ever recovered.

Paul himself was deeply traumatized by his experience, and turned to drink and drugs as an escape. In 1981, at the age of twenty-three, he was found unconscious and had to be rushed to hospital. He had slipped into a coma, and didn't start coming out of it until six weeks later. His recovery was a very long, slow process, and he was left almost blind. He is still struggling to overcome his disabilities today.

# On the run

On February 4, 1974, two British police officers stepped off a plane at Gatwick Airport, just outside London. They were tired, and very depressed. They certainly didn't want to talk to the sea of journalists waiting for them.

"Where is he then?"

"Did you lose him?"

"Have you *slipped up*, Slipper?"

The first of the police officers, Superintendent Jack Slipper, had worked tirelessly for eleven years to catch one of Britain's most notorious criminals – the Great Train Robber, Ronnie Biggs. This moment, stepping off the plane, was supposed to have been Slipper's greatest triumph. Instead, it was the greatest humiliation of his career. Having finally tracked his man down in Brazil, Biggs had slipped through Slipper's fingers; the Brazilian authorities had refused to hand him over. Ronnie Biggs was still a free man – and many people in Britain thought he should remain so.

The relationship between criminals, the public and the police is not always a straightforward one. This seems to be particularly the case with robbers.

"Robbing the rich to give to the poor" has tended to turn villains into heroes, as the stories of Robin Hood show. Ronnie Biggs was no Robin Hood, but many people saw him as a hero all the same, and many were happy when Sergeant Slipper returned to Britain without him. Why? What did Biggs do to deserve it? All he did was rob a train – and get away with it… or is it really that simple?

Ronnie Biggs was always in trouble. Even as a teenager, he was already on the wrong side of the law. He was a thief, and not a very good one, either. He served his first prison sentence in 1949, when he was only nineteen. He stole cars, robbed shops and houses – and, very often, he got caught. Going to prison became rather a habit.

For about ten years, Ronnie was in and out of prison. While he was there, he met other criminals – criminals who had been involved in bigger, more serious crimes than he had. He became good friends with some of them, and they were to play a massive role in shaping the rest of his life. He also learned carpentry skills, and began to think that he might quite enjoy being a carpenter instead of a robber.

By 1959, Ronnie had met his wife, Charmian, and he began to settle down to a quieter life. He did well as a carpenter and decided to set up a little business of his own. He and Charmian had two sons and, for the next three years, all was well – it looked at last as though he might be going straight.

But Ronnie still had his criminal past, and his criminal friends, and in 1963 his friend Bruce Reynolds made him an offer he couldn't refuse.

Two gangs of professional criminals were joining up for one of the biggest robberies in history. The plan: to rob the mail train on the Glasgow to London route, when it was carrying a huge consignment of cash. The haul could be enormous, and Ronnie's heart beat faster at the thought of all that money.

"You can join in if you get us a train driver," Bruce said to Ronnie. "But you'll need to make sure he's tough enough. We don't want anyone who'll crack up under pressure."

"And what do I get?" asked Ronnie. "An equal share?"

"Equal share for you," agreed Bruce. "£40,000 for the driver."

Ronnie's mouth began to water. Yes, he'd gone straight. He'd left the life of crime. But this - well, it could sort him out for life - no more worries about his business, or looking after his family...

"I'll find a driver," he said. "In fact, I know just the man."

It just so happened that Ronnie was doing some carpentry work for a retired train driver. It's not clear what his real name was because he was never caught. So, in this story, we'll call him Dave. Dave's eyes lit up at the idea of earning £40,000 - it was after all an incredible sum, about £500,000 in today's money. He'd do anything for that – even rob a bank! He assured Ronnie that he'd do the job and keep completely quiet afterwards. Ronnie trusted him. Dave was on the job.

The robbery was a massive operation, much bigger than anything Ronnie had been involved in before. In fact he was out of his league, playing along with much more hardened criminals. But there was no turning back. On Tuesday August 6, 1963, Ronnie made his way into London to join up with some of the gang.

From London, the men drove out to an isolated farm in Buckinghamshire. Leatherslade Farm was their base – a place to hide before the robbery, and a place to return to with all the cash. In the course of that day, all sixteen gang members gathered there, ready to move into action.

The next night, they received the news they were waiting for. The mail train was on its way – with a *big* load of cash. In the early hours of the morning, the men piled into their vehicles, and set off. Ronnie's role in the robbery was going to be simple: he had to keep Dave happy, and make sure the old man was in the right place at the right time.

The plan was this. Two of the robbers would stop the train by fiddling with signal lights along the route, turning one amber, and the next one red. Some of the other robbers would overpower the driver. Another group would uncouple the engine and the front cars (the ones containing the cash). Dave would then drive these forward to a bridge up ahead, leaving the rest of the train (containing Post Office workers and mail) behind.

At the bridge, the gang would form a chain to unload the sacks of cash, loading them as fast as they could into a waiting truck and Land Rovers. Then they'd be off – into the night with their loot, back to the safety of Leatherslade Farm.

It all went according to plan – almost. The train stopped at the red light, and the robbers quickly climbed on board. They hadn't expected the driver to put up a fight, and they hadn't planned on using violence. But the driver *did* resist – and one of the robbers hit him over the head. He was not badly hurt, but this act was to have far-reaching consequences for the robbers later on.

At this point, Ronnie Biggs brought Dave to the engine, so that he could drive it forward to the bridge. Dave looked shocked to see Jack Mills, the driver, with blood on his face, but there was no time to worry about it.

"Get this thing moving!" one of the robbers instructed him.

When Dave didn't start the train quickly enough, he was shoved out of the way and Jack Mills was put back in the driver's seat. The train shunted forward to the bridge.

At the bridge, Ronnie took Dave away, while the

rest of the gang unloaded the money. From here on, everything went according to plan. As dawn began to break, the robbers were back at Leatherslade Farm, with their vehicles hidden out of sight.

Exhilarated, the robbers counted the money. It was a staggering sum – £2,631,784. That's almost £30 million pounds in today's money. Carefully, they divided it up, listening all the while on the radio for news of the robbery. It didn't take long. The police were soon on the case, hunting for the most successful train robbers of all time.

But the success didn't last. Within a couple of days, things began to go wrong. The robbers had planned to stay at the farm for about a week, but they heard on the news that the police were going to search the whole area thoroughly. They had to get out. And so they dispersed quickly, all disappearing back to their separate homes and families. They were still confident that they'd pulled it off.

But they had made a crucial mistake. They knew that all the evidence sitting at the farm had to be destroyed. They were relying on someone else to come in after they had gone, to clean up – and burn the whole place down, if necessary. Instead, this person pocketed what he'd been paid to do the job, and disappeared. So, when the police found Leatherslade Farm, they knew they'd struck lucky. It was, as one of them said, "one big clue."

It wasn't long before the police had a good idea of

who was responsible. There were fingerprints everywhere. Ronnie Biggs had left his on a Monopoly board, and on a bottle of tomato sauce. And because most of the robbers had been in trouble before, the police had a copy of their fingerprints on file. One by one, they were found and hauled in for questioning, and Ronnie's turn came along with everyone else. Only four out of the sixteen men were never caught – including Dave, the train driver who'd been hired for the robbery.

When it came to the trial, the robbers stood little chance of being let off. The evidence stacked up against them and, to make matters worse, Jack Mills, the train driver, appeared as a witness. His bandaged head spoke volumes, making the robbers look ruthless and dangerous, even though most of them had committed no violence at all. No one was surprised at the string of "Guilty" verdicts.

But the robbers' sentences caused shock waves across the country. The judge took the whole thing very seriously indeed, and most of the robbers, including Ronnie himself, were sentenced to thirty years in prison. Thirty years! It was more than many criminals received for cold-blooded murder. So, as soon as they were transferred to prison, many of the robbers were thinking of only one thing: escape.

Ronnie himself was sent to Wandsworth Prison in London. At first, he had no intention of trying to escape. He had heard that a new parole system was soon going to be set up, which would mean that he might be let out after ten years. But, even so, ten years was a long time, and there was no guarantee that the new system would be running in the near future. It wasn't long before he began to think of an escape route.

There were plenty of people in Wandsworth Prison who were more than willing to give Ronnie a helping hand. In fact, one man named Paul was rather an expert at escapes, and helped persuade Ronnie to go for it. And there was another man named Eric who, with a sentence of twelve years, was just as eager to escape as Ronnie was. So together they devised a plan. Every day, the prisoners were allowed an hour's exercise in the prison yard. The wall surrounding the yard was the only barrier between them and freedom, but it was 25 feet high. Ronnie would have to get over it somehow – but how?

Obviously, he'd need outside help, but that wasn't a problem. Eric was allowed regular visits from friends and family, so he used them as a go-between, carrying information in and out of the prison. Moreover, Paul was soon going to be released and would be able to organize the whole operation from the outside once he was free again. It was a huge risk, but helping one of the train robbers to escape struck him as a risk worth taking. After all, there was bound to be something in it for him.

Ronnie and Eric knew they also needed *inside*

help from fellow prisoners who could be trusted. That wasn't a problem either, for there were plenty of men who were willing to get involved. Ronnie picked two helpers and swore them to secrecy. They now had everything they needed.

The plan was daring. *Very* daring. But, on July 8, 1965, this is what happened. At 3:10pm, Ronnie and Eric were in the exercise yard, walking around as usual. They heard the sound of a large vehicle pulling up on the other side of the wall. This was followed by the sight of two rope ladders appearing over the top. Ronnie and Eric sprinted for them, while their inside helpers dived to stop the prison officers from reaching them.

On the other side of the wall there was a furniture van with a hole cut in its roof. Inside the van there were lots of mattresses, so that when the men jumped down they wouldn't hurt themselves. The plan worked like a dream! In seconds, Ronnie and Eric were down the other side and into a getaway car. They'd done it!

The problem with escaping, however, is not breaking free, but *staying* free. Several of the other train robbers managed to escape in the next couple of years, but none of them managed to remain on the loose. Ronnie Biggs now had the greatest challenge ahead of him. With his name and photograph splashed across all the newspapers in England, it would be very difficult to avoid detection for long.

The only option he had, was to go overseas, possibly for good.

After staying in hiding for a while, Ronnie started using his share of the loot to create a new life for himself. First, he paid a special criminal organization to smuggle him into France. This organization was able to arrange everything he needed - transport, a fake passport and a whole new identity. And, once in Paris, he took a very drastic step - he actually changed the way he looked, with plastic surgery. With a different-shaped nose and a face-lift, you would have to look twice before realizing that this was the same Ronnie Biggs as the one in the newspapers. So far, so good. But it wasn't safe to stay in France, all the same. To stay on the loose, he'd have to go further.

With another forged passport and another new identity, Ronnie made his way to Australia, where he thought he might be safe. His wife Charmian and his children also adopted new identities and joined him. Ronnie's loot soon ran out, but he found work very easily and, for a while, he and his family were able to settle down. No one was likely to guess the real identity of Mr. Terence King in this vast new land. Or were they?

If Ronnie had been the only train robber, he might have been able to stay in Australia, undetected, for many years. But, back in England, fresh news began to break. First, another escapee named Charlie Wilson was recaptured in Canada. Then Bruce

Reynolds, Ronnie's friend, was captured too. The news reminded everyone that there was another robber on the run, and Ronnie Biggs was soon in all the newspapers all over again. He was featured in Australian magazines, too, and even with the face-lift, the pictures looked remarkably similar to Mr. Terence King. People who recognized him set the stories flying that he was hiding in Australia, and the police were quick to pick them up. Before he knew it, Ronnie Biggs was on the run again.

With the help of a friend's passport (which had its photograph carefully exchanged for one of Ronnie), Ronnie became Michael Haynes and headed for Brazil. He had to leave Charmian and the children behind, because the police had realized who, and where, she was. But this was it: a boat to Panama, followed by a plane to Rio de Janeiro. He arrived on March 11, 1970, and there he stayed.

The years drifted by, and Ronnie remained on the loose in Brazil, with few people really knowing who he was. He befriended a woman named Raimunda, and they became lovers. Little did he know what a big role she was going to play in his life.

In Britain, news of the train robbers was no longer hitting the headlines. Ronnie had now been free for so long that many people wished him luck. Over time, the legend of the train robber on the loose developed a romantic appeal – he had done so well to escape, and a life on the run seemed daring and adventurous. Above all, people seem to have a grudging respect for someone who had managed to escape detection for over ten years. Surely it wasn't worth chasing him any longer?

But the police were still determined to catch him, and newspapers were still interested in tracking him down – if only for a great story. And, in the end, it was a British newspaper that set the police onto his trail.

A friend of Ronnie's known as Conti, one of the few people who knew where he was, talked to a journalist from the *Daily Express* in London and revealed that he knew Ronnie's whereabouts. The journalist, Colin Mackenzie, was very excited. It would be a massive scoop to tell his story. Knowing that secrecy was essential, he spoke to Ronnie on the phone and checked that he was who Conti said he was. Ronnie agreed to give his story for a fee, and in early 1974 Colin flew to Brazil to meet Ronnie personally. He agreed to pay £35,000.

What Ronnie didn't know was that Colin had already betrayed Ronnie to his bosses – and his bosses had betrayed him even further and had gone straight to the police at Scotland Yard. They had no intention of paying the £35,000, and Colin was not the only man to get on a plane to Rio de Janeiro. Superintendent Jack Slipper was on his way, too.

So how did Ronnie avoid being taken back to Britain in handcuffs? The answer lay in Brazilian law. No man who had fathered a Brazilian child could be forced to leave the country. And, just before the arrival of Jack Slipper, Ronnie's girlfriend Raimunda had discovered she was pregnant. As a result, Ronnie Biggs was given the right to remain in Brazil for the rest of his life.

So there Ronnie stayed, for many, many years, out of reach of the British justice system. Raimunda had a son, and he was named Michael. Now that his location was known, Ronnie became rather a celebrity. He wrote several books, including *Odd Man Out* and *Ronnie Biggs: His Own Story*, which were both accounts of the train robbery and his eventful life on the run. Many other accounts of his life have been written, too, including one about Jack Slipper's failed attempt to haul him back to Britain.

Ultimately, though, Ronnie Biggs longed to return to Britain, even knowing that if he did so, he would have to hand himself over to the police. Eventually, on May 7, 2001, having suffered from a number of strokes, this is what he did. He was arrested immediately and taken to prison, despite his failing health. At the time of writing, he is seventy-three years old and in Belmarsh Prison, although he has been rushed to Woolwich Hospital on a number of occasions. His son Michael continues to campaign for his release.

# TRUE ESCAPE STORIES

**Paul Dowswell**

Finally, the night had come to take a trip to the roof. Morris spent the day beforehand trying to curb his restlessness. What if the way up to the roof was blocked? What if the ventilator motor had been replaced after all? All their painstaking work would be wasted. The 12-year sentence stretched out before him. Then another awful thought occurred. The holes in the wall would be discovered eventually, and that would mean even more years added on to his sentence.

As well as locked doors, high walls and barbed wire, many escaping prisoners also face savage dogs and armed guards who shoot to kill. From Alcatraz to Devil's Island, read the extraordinary tales of people who risked their lives for their freedom.

# TRUE
# SURVIVAL
# STORIES

**Paul Dowswell**

As he fell through the floor Griffiths instinctively grabbed at the bombsight with both hands, but an immense gust of freezing air sucked the rest of his body out of the aircraft. With the wind and the throb of the Boston's two engines roaring in his ears, he found himself halfway out of the plane, legs and lower body pressed hard against the fuselage. He yelled at the top of his voice: "Geeeerrroooooowwww!!!!", but knew immediately that there was almost no chance his crewmate could hear him.

From shark attacks and blazing airships to exploding spacecraft and sinking submarines, these are real stories of people who have stared death in the face and lived to tell the tale. Find out what separates the living from the dead when catastrophe strikes.